Dominate Your Ground

Dominate Your Ground

Mark I'Anson

Contents

1   Introduction

First of all, thank you for buying my book. I've been meaning to write it for a couple of years and I did start it but, well...business and life got in the way. So, my first attempt turned into an instruction manual, which many of you may already have.

Dominate Your Ground is about a journey, part story, part 'how to' so you can learn from some of my mistakes. If you'd like to add some of your own experiences, I'd be glad to hear from you so I can add them to my next book.

There are 'thinkers' and 'doers' (and a mixture of both) in the world, I'm a *doer*, I do a lot – I've been blessed with some sort of fantastic energy which I love. But, there's a problem with *doers* (as my wife will tell you) in that, *doers* don't plan well. We spend all of our time doing so we make mistakes..... *doers* make lots of mistakes.

I'm not judging anyone for being a *thinker* or a *doer* but, just be aware of which you are. Of course, things aren't as black and white as that but, forgive me for my slight autism breaking out there. Everyone has a little autism in them, some call it character, others might call it personality but, mine shows itself in my black and white/right or wrong thinking. For my brain, there are rules, and I find it difficult to break my rules.

Nothing, for me, is grey but luckily I'm reasonably intelligent and understand that the world is in fact mixtures of grey. I'm also of a military background and that early career suited my younger mind – things in the Army are often black & white. I was either right or wrong, my commanding officer was nearly always right – that's how it works in the military. How else would you get young men and women to fight conflict in countries that some have never heard of, obeying orders they often don't understand..?

You may be a freer thinker than I – be thankful for that - but, to succeed, you have to 'do'. There is not much point reading this book (or my other book), if you are only going to think about it – it's about doing. I may take something I heard a good friend of mine, Rob Moore say "don't spend all of your time getting perfect, start doing and get perfect later".

So, this book isn't for the shelf, it's written so you can start doing. You'll make mistakes along the way. I make loads; managing those mistakes is the art. Make your mistakes small and almost painless, learn from them and do better next time.

It's called 'doing' and learning from mistakes to grow, I should think of a great quote but, for the moment, I'll just stick to that.

I went on to complete an engineering apprenticeship after school, and educated myself late with the Open University – some would say that I'm not a writer but, that's the weird thing about doers – I'm not too worried about what qualifications I have, I just started writing – so, I guess that I am a writer!

If you would like further coaching on 'doing' – ask me about my coaching days. They are non-technical, will push you and challenge you to do – even for the thinkers out there…

Everything mentioned in this book is available from my online store – all of the paperwork, spread sheets, scripts, contracts – the lot..!

It would have been difficult to put everything mentioned actually in the book as some tools are spread sheets, PowerPoint templates, Word documents etc. So the store has been set so you can get hold of them easily, in their original format. A link to the store is at the end of the book.

I've included a few 'Tasks' for you to do along the way. They don't cost a lot and they won't take up a lot of your time but, they will help you on your journey. Do the tasks, in any order and feel free to give me your thoughts and feedback.

1.1 A bit about property

There are tons of other books, courses and workshops on the different strategies and it's not the place of this book to go into them, it would take forever.

Whatever strategy you've chosen – this book will complement them all, whether you're building a portfolio for yourself or with partners, you'll still need leads. The leads you get won't all fit into your idea of a deal. But, don't worry, as they are still valuable as tradable entities. We won't be looking for particular types of property or deals; we'll be looking for sellers, people who we can help out of a situation. The property (at this point) is largely irrelevant. If you're keeping them, only buy the ones you want, or that fit your strategy, the rest can be traded to others to keep the cash flowing.

So everything that I'll go through in this book will complement every other strategy, it is not stand alone. Getting leads, converting deals and trading property will make you money and that's why you bought the book, right?

Leads – Deals - Trades

Keeping the deals will create wealth using 'leverage' – the leverage of other people's money. If you buy and use some funds, 25% at the moment will secure an asset which is worth four times the amount you put in. The growth (or profit) will be on the greater amount, not just your 25%. The growth is on the value of the asset. If you keep them long enough, you'll create your own wealth as long they cash flow positively along the way.

Many things use leverage to make money, businesses use the skills and time of others, you can leverage stocks to trade but, property is one of the easiest to understand. That's what makes property attractive.

1.2 A bit about buying & trading properties

I'll tell you more about the trading later in the book. There are lots of different strategies out there but I'll be focusing on buying at a discount and lease option strategies mainly because they are the easiest to sell onto another investor.

Before you try them, it's worth getting some education on how each one is used. I run workshops mainly in the Midlands and London; feel free to enquire about them. Property education shouldn't be expensive to learn a strategy unless you'd like hand holding through the processes, then it can be more expensive.

Workshops are generally more affordable, a great time to network, learn and discover if a particular strategy is for you. Plus, you can ask as many questions as you want.

The idea is that you keep the leads or deals that you want and trade the rest bringing in cashflow for you.

1.3   A bit more about me

That little bit in the beginning where I tell you about me – I started my adult life in the Armed Forces, I served 12 years in the British Army, had an excellent time, met some great people that are still friends today. I travelled across the world, drove big and fast things, jumped off (and out) of things, blew stuff up, saw some action, and was decorated for my efforts.

When I left, I felt like I was on leave and even when I started in my mundane, civilian job with my mundane civilian car, it didn't feel right. I wanted more…

Don't get me wrong, the jobs were okay and I have never had a sob story. I had a decent upbringing, loving parents, good schools but, I always thought that successful careers might make you financially stable but, they will never make you financially free.

Jump forward a few years and I was living the high life, selling international property, everyone wore big watches, flash suits and pointy shoes. Many trips to Cyprus, Spain and South Africa, so that my life seemed to revolve around airports, hotels and glitzy shows.

Everyone felt the need to show off how successful they were. Then, the crash came in 2008 and the international property scene all but, disappeared. There was unease in my office, I felt like I was starting all over again. During 2008, people were keeping their 'hard earned' in their pockets in case of stormy times ahead.

I'd traded property for a long time and worked in the background as a supplier to quite a few big marketing agents. I learned my trade, made mistakes along the way but, decided to exit the international scene altogether. When I say that I decided, really, it was decided for me.

The best decision was honing my skills, back to the UK and specialising – focus on one area, grabbing bargain properties and trading them on. This book will show you how it's done, it's a part of my journey – it's been a great one but, bumpy along the way.

I am dedicating this book to every single person that's helped me on my journey and continues to do so. You are all fabulous, the people that have trusted me with their audiences, my clients (some of which I can call friends), my suppliers, my loving wife who has stood by me and seen my successes and mistakes, if you don't have a reason why – put down this book, pack up and do something else. It's going to be a ride; I'm not saying that it's going to be easy; I'm saying that it's going to be worth it...

Let's crack on with the content, as John Cox (Host of the Bucks Property Meet) continues to remind me, we gotta have great content...

2   Dominate Your Ground

A good place to start would be to explain the title; Dominate Your Ground is taken from a military term that's used in times of conflict. Infantry soldiers take over a building to set up a base and organise patrols from that base. The patrols get bigger and wider and restrict enemy movement in the territory, in effect – Dominating the Ground.

Whilst running sales teams in various businesses, I have used the similar tactics to make sure that we were getting the maximum possible business from a patch, controlling the area, restricting the competitor's movements, gaining and growing more business.

Apologies in advance of my various uses of the terms: Area, Territory, Patch and Ground – they all mean the same thing.

2.1 Who are your Targets?

Let's start with why people will sell their property to you, as opposed to the local estate agent.

You'll be a "solution" company, working with your vendors to find the best solution for whatever situation they might find themselves in, and find the best outcome for them and their family. It may be something that you do directly, or may be recommendations and advice that lead them to an alternative route to solving their problems. At this stage, we're not looking for property, we're looking for people.

Most vendors need to sell for one or many of the following reasons:

2.1.1 Mortgage Arrears

Many people fall behind on their mortgage payments through no fault of their own. Unexpected illness, unemployment, bereavement, an increase in interest rates etc. are all things we have no control over and can cause havoc on finances. Soon they fall into arrears and run the risk of being repossessed. You can help by keeping or trading the property using the equity (or your deal) to get them out of that situation.

2.1.2 Financial Difficulties

Mounting debts on credit cards and loans can catch people off guard and can put a strain on their finances, leaving less money at the end of the month to live. If they can't pay their bills they may lose their home through bankruptcy. You can help by managing their situation and stopping any bankruptcy orders against them.

2.1.3 Chain Breaks

One in every three property transactions in the UK falls through because of buyers pulling out at the last minute. They might have already committed to buying their next home but can't move until their property has been sold. This holds everything up and can become a nightmare for everyone involved. You can help by buying directly from them and allowing the purchase of their next home to continue.

2.1.4 Divorce

Many couples own their home in joint names with both listed on the mortgage. Divorce often forces one party to buy the other's share but going via an estate agent can take too long and is not guaranteed. People just want to get on with their lives as quickly as possible without any delays. You can help by buying their property quickly from them releasing the equity to pay for their ex partner's share.

2.1.5 Relocation

People's jobs change and sometime require them to move to a different city or country which can be a very stressful experience. Trying to sell their property before they go in a short space of time is something they could do without. They've got quite enough to worry about anyway. You can help by buying their property quickly, releasing the equity to pay for their new home. Depending on when they need to move you can let them stay in their home until they relocate.

2.1.6 Problem Property

Their property has been on the market for some time and they just can't sell it. They've dropped the price and put it on with multiple agents yet they've had no offers. They've had enough and you just want to move on. The reason for not selling may be that it's overpriced or that it has problems with it that are putting potential buyers off. You can help by buying their property quickly from them allowing them to move on.

2.1.7 Inheritance Tax

They might have inherited a property and want to sell it. This may be to pay the inheritance tax at 40% if the whole estate is worth over £325,000 (2009 – 2015 rates) or just that they would like to sell the property quickly and easily.

If they've inherited a property where the value the estate is over £300,000 (2007-2008), they could be required to pay tax of 40% within 6 months following the death. Not everyone has to pay inheritance tax and a solicitor should be consulted for more information. You can help by buying their property quickly, releasing the equity to pay the inheritance tax.

2.2 Find your Ground

Let's choose the area first. It is good practice to think about your local area, I realise that some areas are better than others but, where yields are low, or discounts not quite there, try to think outside the box a little.

In the early days of 'Buy to Let', before we all got educated about property, most of us got into property in an accidental way, we stumbled upon a deal and that got our mind working. Could there be more opportunities like this out there?

Nowadays, it's considered good practice to work your own area. Trying to manage a patch that is miles away will test you, it's not forgiving, and the travelling doesn't get easier. You should value your time and travelling takes that time away. It's not productive time either, some will argue that you can listen to CD's and make it productive but, working in your business is productive, driving generally isn't – no matter how you try to justify it.

Think about the wear and tear on you as well as your vehicle and the erosion of your valuable time. You got into this to improve your quality of life, not to buy yourself another job.

If you're serious and genuinely convinced that your area won't work (and I seriously doubt that), then move into one that does. You are a property person now; we move to suit our business if we need to.

A suitable area depends on how you'll be building your portfolio. Let's start with the simplest, Below Market Value (BMV) offers using straight purchases.

A BMV patch is helping those people in our society that 'topple over' in financial terms. These types of deals aren't found in 'up market' estates with double fronted houses stood at the end of grand, gravel, gated driveways.

Those that topple financially are found in terraces, those 'laddered' streets of Victorian houses in towns with lower demographic customers. You will be looking for a few key pointers, the white vans of the gardeners, electricians, decorators and the like. The area will have a few betting shops, pubs, and corner shops, the lower priced supermarkets like Aldi and Lidl.

I'll go into that more later, for now let's think about those areas. You'll be looking for an area with around 4,000 houses. There's no point trying to dominate the whole city before you've even got a leaflet printed. Businesses in the area have been marketing in the area since it was built and they didn't start by taking it over on day one.

I was speaking at a property meeting in Central London last year and when I've finished my talks, some of the audience come up to chat with me to find out more. On this occasion, the chap asked what the best marketing strategy was for getting leads and I asked him what patch he was working.

His reply made me chuckle, "Oh, South London." I said, without a hint of irony. "What, all of it?" He said. "Yeah, anything in South London is fine."

I had to think about that, just for a second, the chap was not only trying to market to nearly four million people but, also any type of property. It would take an absolute fortune to dominate this type of area, and property. It's too broad a strategy; you're not trying to take over the world, just your patch.

The whole of America is littered with failed English businesses that thought, there's such an amazing amount of people that it would be impossible to fail. In reality, people buy local when they can. It is the same here...

2.2.1 Start with Local – Stick to Local

The Ordnance Survey in this country have produced some of the best maps in the world so, they have already done some of the work for you. The OS 1:25,000 maps go down to house level. Although Google Street View may have been a revelation when introduced, in reality, there's nothing better than a good scale, paper map to choose a patch as Google decided that they'd map to street level, not house level – it's the houses I'm after, not the streets.

A map is an illustration of an aerial view, not a picture and it's worth bearing that in mind. Roads and streets are represented by coloured lines, buildings by symbol. Although drawn to scale, maps are not entirely to scale, a church building is not 100m across as the symbol would suggest.

A 1:25,000 map will show the shapes of the houses, their configuration around a town. I'll give an example of that – terraced houses are drawn as rectangular blocks on a map, their gardens are drawn by thin black lines. The distance from the road is visible too.

The laddered streets of terraced housing can be easily seen on these types of maps, areas can be plotted using the natural boundaries of the area. A large road, a river, an industrial area can form a boundary to your patch.

It pays to do some research first though, just to check before you start drawing all over your maps.

The map is the start of the research, if you operate in a patch that you already know, and then you'll have an advantage. I was speaking with a couple recently; they lived in London and had heard that Norwich was a good area to work. They'd done the research and were preparing to move up to Norwich.

As the conversation progressed, it's turns out that one half of the couple, Emma was from Australia and had lived in Stevenage for 10 years. Steve and Emma met in Stevenage where he grew up, although they now lived in London.

I asked what was wrong with Stevenage. The reply I got back was that they thought Norwich might be better after doing the research.

A better patch, is the one you know – every time, all of the time – I can't make this any clearer, if you have lived somewhere for 10 years, or grown up in a town or area, that's your patch. You already have a distinct advantage over anyone doing a bit of research on the internet or advice by any training company.

Your patch is the area you know – you'll already know the estates to avoid, you'll already know where the 'clues' are that people have toppled over in financial terms. You'll know which factories are about to close making hundreds of people redundant.

Living in an area for any length of time is research and there is no better research – don't let anyone tell you differently.

I started my 'patch' work in an area where I grew up, I moved back into it. The next patch I worked was in an area that I lived, well around a mile away. Making mistakes is what I do best but, the mistakes I make don't cost me very much. It's a darn sight less painful making mistakes in a patch I know than one I don't. I learn quicker and cheaper, and that, I like.

TASK

Pop into a Waterstones or WHSmith and buy a map – the exact one is an Ordnance Survey Explorer with an orange cover. The scale is 1:25,000

When you've opened your map out on the kitchen table, have a look at the symbols box and start to figure out what each means. Symbols for railway lines are thin, solid black lines and the train stations are red circles. Rivers are blue lines, with lakes being bigger areas of blue; you'll soon get the picture.

A map is an aerial representation of the ground, it's not a picture so everything on it, aren't exactly to scale.

If it's your home town or 'patch' map, the next thing to look at are the houses. Terraced houses look like ladders, even their gardens will be there too.

The bigger houses will be set back from the road a little and have bigger gardens; the estates will have less straight roads and cul de sacs.

A BMV patch of 4,000 houses will be around the size of two 50p pieces, a lease option patch will be four 50p pieces as a rough guide.

See if you can find 1, 2 or 3 possible areas on the map. Then, go out and have a drive around each of the areas. Are there other key features in any of the areas that might make them more attractive? Is one of the areas better than the others? Go back to the map and see if you can now spot these factors on the map.

2.2.2 Research – Using the Research of Others

There's a wonderful company called CACI and they do research on the ground in tremendous detail. Lots of large companies use them before siting their businesses, health clubs, supermarkets, chain stores, franchises and loads more.

I used to work for a company that sold scanners to NHS and private hospitals. The company would buy a CACI report when deciding to site a new scanner. These things (the scanners) cost around £1.5m each and had to have a building built around them for another £160,000 and then employ three staff for another £200,000pa so the siting was important to get the best 'customer' (patient) foot fall.

A report would drill down into the area, giving guidelines on the demographics of an area, right down to the amount of credit cards in each household. Fabulous research, very detailed and it allowed us, as a company, to decide the best site for a scanner.

The thing we were looking for was lots of sick NHS patients – you may think that there's more money in private medical work but, I assure you, there's a lot of money providing medical services to the NHS and they have an abundance of sick people. The thing is, we didn't want middle class estates or chocolate box villages, the areas that gave us the best bang for our buck were lower demographic areas. Those areas had NHS cover, not private healthcare and they got sicker more often.

The problem for a start-up is that the research isn't cheap however, you can still benefit from other businesses that have already paid for this research.

We are a Tesco family although if there is a special occasion or we just fancy a treat, then we may splash out and go to Waitrose. But our main weekly shop is Tesco and I presume that most of my readers are similar (other mid-range supermarkets are available). Those people that I can help don't shop in Waitrose at all, and sometimes, they do not even shop at Tesco.

I've often used Asda as an example. Walk into an Asda store and look, I mean, really look at the layout of the store. I'm from an upper working class/lower middle class background and upbringing, my family is a meat and two veg type family, we don't have soft drinks in the house, we eat sensibly, exercise well and I'd like to think that we were brought up right.

When checking the layout of the store in your local area, what do you see first? In supermarkets that we shop in, I expect to be greeted with a huge fruit and vegetable section at the entrance. It's inviting, and it seems to make sense to my upbringing. Those stores that have clothing at the entrance, or offers on crates of beer, or a huge pastry section don't seem to look right.

Don't take my word for it either, try this for yourself. Have a trip out to a few stores that are on your prospective patch – you'll be surprised.

The supermarkets are big business and they set out their stores to suit their customers. They do it well, and leave no stone unturned in seeking out ways of squeezing that extra 50p out of a sale with an offer, a deal for their customers based on their extensive analysis.

Of course, don't rely on this alone; check out what else is in the area. There are a few clues that can swing the research. I'm looking for those clues such as Cash Converter stores, the betting shops, the scruffier pubs. If they are combined with a smaller, lower priced supermarket like Aldi or Lidl, I'm starting to think that I'm in the right place for a BMV patch.

In a BMV patch, I'm looking for those that that sometimes topple over in financial terms, and if I produce enough leads I can be choosy with them. I'll explain more about that later.

Just to recap, I've found a lower tier (in price) big supermarket and a cheaper smaller supermarkets serving the same community, then I've found the lower demographic shops. These are 'out of town' as the shops in town centres don't count as these are serving the whole town, and not just my patch.

At this point I'm just looking for a BMV patch of around 4,000 houses, I'm not looking to take over the world as I'll make some mistakes. These mistakes won't cost much in terms of my marketing spend as the area is small, so I'm managing my mistakes – they'll be a few.

I've confirmed the area on the ground; next stop is the maps to draw out the boundaries of the area. Boundaries could be large roads, rivers, industrial areas; they are obvious when you're looking from above. On a 1:25,000 scale OC Map, 4,000 houses takes up around two 50p pieces in area.

Later on, I'll be running through the pillars of support as a marketing strategy but, the idea of pulling in leads from a patch is simple. The only point of advertising is to get the phone ring or get the recipient to do something, for example call or text.

Bearing that in mind, you won't be trying to create a national brand; it's costly and pointless at this stage of your business. There isn't a budget for a particular patch because that depends on your own start point. Everything you do to start should be as cheap as possible whilst the mistakes are being made and you are learning.

The idea is to make your mistakes cheap whilst you put systems in place. Once your systems are in place, you can expand having not run out of funds before you get your first deal to the table.

It's common to imagine that 'carpet bombing' a whole town will bring in leads but, marketing doesn't work like that. Potential customers have to see your marketing a few times (some say seven) before they'll act on it.

2.3 Choose Your Tactics

When applying the foundations, it important to note that they work together – I promise you that if you only use one method, you'll get no calls and no leads. Marketing is an art form; one method doesn't work better than another in that they all have pros and cons. Some cost mainly in time, some in money, and others in effort. The methods that I'll go through that cost in money may also cost in time and effort – make your own decisions on which ones to try first and how much to spend – your budget is your own and only you can tell how much to put into each and when you've run out.

I've included ten strategies below; you don't have to use them all. Use three or four of them together, make small mistakes along the way and remember to test, measure and evaluate the results.

2.3.1 Cards in Businesses

This has got to be the cheapest method, has been used for years and works, if it's done properly. Some will say (the people that are not doing it) that it will cost 50p per week to place a card on a pin board or window of some businesses. And, by that, I mean the following – chip shops, Post Offices, newsagents, betting shops, corner shops and the like.

You won't be putting a few in; you'll be putting a card in EVERY business that will have one. Once you go round and talk to business owners, you'll soon discover that a lot will let you put a card up for free – it doesn't get cheaper than that...

Some won't let you put one up at all, that's fine too. This is why you should visit every single business, the more you ask, the more cards you get displayed. This takes a little persistence as business owners won't always be in when you call. The shop assistant has the decision making authority whilst an owner is away but, that authority only allows them to say no, not yes. If you ask a shop assistant that says no, go back and make sure you keep going back until you actually get the owner in.

Although this method is free to cheap, it still costs in time, so it has to be weighed up against the alternatives.

Let's do a couple of numbers – how long will it take you to walk round a few shops to have a conversation with the owner? A day, two days..? How many conversations will result in a placed card? 20, 40, 100..?

The more cards you get out will determine how many times your cards are seen – the more they are seen, the more chances you have to get a call. I've seen people putting three or four cards in newsagents and expecting to get calls – it isn't going to happen, there's too much noise around your cards for people to see them. Get 100 cards out and you'll stand a chance of your card being seen. In this 'space' you'll be starting to Dominate Your Ground.

The pitch to a shop owner is simple:

"I'm helping people in the area clear a few debts using the equity in their property. Would be okay to put a card on your pin board/window/wall?"

If an owner asks for payments then offer a few weeks in advance/upfront and agree a timeframe. If they offer to put one for free, then have your card ready in your hand to give them. They've agreed, strike while the iron is hot.

There's debate on whether you should be using hand written cards or printed, and whilst I'm aware that for some 'ugly marketing' (hand written, scruffy text) works. However, for cards in windows, there's nothing to beat clearly written, legible print. It won't attract everyone but, then again, leads are lost from badly written text. Your own views and values will make your decision for you.

I've found that the betting shops seem to pull in more leads than I'd expect, Post Offices are great if the board is sited where the queues form, and useless if it's at the other end of the counter. Every business has a different traffic flow, and that's the real reason why you'll have to get a few out there, they won't all get seen. It's impossible to research every business to watch the traffic flows to test which cards get seen. So, instead, get more cards out and cover more businesses. That way, your mistakes won't have cost much.

The fast food places sometimes have pin boards but, these types of businesses that open only at night time are attracting a younger crowd and not always home owners. It's worthy to note as putting out 30 cards in late night kebab houses might not get you the leads you actually want.

Businesses serving a community are usually sited along a couple of streets and these can work well for you. Do not forget that there are also the 'inner' businesses that are stand alone in their neighbourhoods. These types of businesses are valuable as they directly serve your (potential) customers.

2.3.2 Window 'Sticks'

Whilst you're scouting about popping into businesses and chatting with owners, popping cards all over the place, there's a great strategy for those that will allow and that's called 'window sticks'. I'll explain: Let's say that you are chatting to a newsagent, or any business with a street facing window. If you had a bunch of 'reverse tack' stickers the owner might let you put one of them on the inside of the window.

Reverse tack means that the glue is on the visible side of the leaflet. They are usually made of printed vinyl and so are more expensive than regular leaflets but, there are a few advantages:

- They are vinyl, so writing a post date on them is difficult as it will rub off
- They stay fully coloured for longer
- They work 24 hours a day in busy streets

It would be for you to decide on their worth, should you use them but, for me, they've been invaluable as a lot of businesses will allow you to display them. They need to be no larger than A5 (or even smaller).

If you ask your printer about them, they'll show you the vinyl that they are made from.

2.3.3   Bin Sticks

At the same time as getting the reverse tack stickers for windows, you can ask about getting your leaflets done with adhesive on the regular side.

This next strategy is called 'bin sticks' and if you are pounding the streets during your first few weeks delivering leaflets, you'll come across another *leafleter* doing the same thing.

Bin sticks are just leaflets made and printed in vinyl that your second leaflet guy can stick to bins. In fact, he can follow the bin along his rounds attaching leaflets to any bins out on the pavement.

Be aware though, this could be considered fly posting so please check with your local council and ask them what they consider fly posting. Usually, it means posting on council property, not bins.

The advantages to using this strategy are numerous; they will stay 'readable' for longer than a regular leaflet, they become a 'branding' exercise for anyone than doesn't respond right away but may need your services in the future. And, as they are vinyl, they stay looking good for longer too.

If you ask your leaflet guy to stick 1,000 leaflets, that's around a full day's work but, it's easier work than putting leaflets through letterboxes if they follow the bin men round when all of the bins are out.

TASK

Take out a subscription to one or both of the industry magazines. There's Your Property Network run by Ant Lyons and Property Investor News run by Richard Bowser. In my opinion, they are both quality magazines, each coming from a different angle at the market place.

Magazine subscription isn't expensive and you'll get an overview of the activities of those in the industry. There are articles to educate, adverts from course sellers, 'joint ventures' wanted adverts and case studies by real people doing real stuff in property.

If you needed any inspiration that you're on the right path, then these two publications can provide your monthly 'pep talk'

Stick to your own path though, magazines carry articles different strategies every month and it would be easy to be dazzled into thinking that this month's is a better one than last month – it's not, it's just different.

Now, the hard part of the task! Actually read the magazines – don't just allow them to fall on the mat and then on a shelf. Make sure that you note down useful articles. Maybe keep a journal or notebook in which you jot down ideas on the articles for future reference.

2.3.4 Leaflets

A lot has been written about leaflets over the years and I'll add to it here. Some will tell you that they don't work. "I've tried leaflets and they didn't work for me." I often hear.

It's not the leaflets that didn't work; it's the management of the delivery that didn't work usually. At the start of this book, I mentioned making mistakes, well, here's a chance to make a few small ones without too much pain or expense.

In this section I've written my own experience and just for balance, I thought that I'd get an expert in too. Suzanne Bates runs a property leaflet company called Smart Property Leaflets along with Mark Walker and Andy Haynes, I often refer my coaching clients to them as they produce over 50 ready-made templates to choose from. It seemed only right that I should give my readers both my experience and theirs as experts in their field.

Let's start right at the beginning; one of the earliest references for the use of leaflets that I can find is 1592 by a chap called Richard Burbage. He owned the Curtain Theatre in Shoreditch, London and to drive people into the theatre to watch his new plays, he used leaflets and fly posters all around London.

Leaflets have been around ever since, used in slightly different ways but, essentially the same. They've always been printed or hand written on *holdable* sized paper, nearly always been shoved through letterboxes. If anyone tells you they don't work – have a little giggle to yourself and tell them, "Well, they've worked since Shakespeare's day".

A4 is the most common size of leaflet that comes through most letterboxes but smaller businesses often use A5 (myself included) as they're less expensive and lighter so the carriage is less too. If you use a local printer, the carriage doesn't matter but, the printing cost might.

Make the middle light coloured – this seems obvious to me (as a photographer) but, I'll explain why. Artists and photographers produce an image and they want their viewer to look 'into' the image, protect their eyes from wandering outside the borders of their work. This is why borders work, most paintings, and photographs use darker borders to keep the viewer's eyes inside the work. Photographs in galleries, paintings, advertising pictures, even televisions have dark borders for the same reason.

There's two ways to go here, the centre of the leaflet should be light in colour or your leaflet should have a dark border – I'll let you choose which way you go but, choose one or the other.

Next step – we've got to choose the wording, most advertisers will agree that they follow the AIDA Model:

- **A**ttention
- **I**nterest
- **D**esire
- **A**ction

It's not new, it's been around for years and used by internet marketers, print advertisers and all forms of adverts, the world over.

BMV Patch

The attention grabber should be big, bold type – Need to Sell Your House? Stuck in Debt? Debt Worries? Can't Pay the Mortgage? Facing Repossession?

Any of the above will work as attention grabbers – I use one on my set of three bandit boards which simply says – **READ THIS SIGN**. It's just to grab attention to your advert and nothing more.

Next part of the leaflet should build some interest and desire in what you have to say – your message, how you can help the viewer. A few features and benefits of your service based on what your viewer might want. How you can help them.

- Houses Bought Fast
- Quick Decisions
- Confidential
- All Considered
- Any Price
- Any Area

All of these work as interest and desire builders.

The last part of the leaflet should contain the Call to Action – what do you want your viewer to do next? Text a number, call a number? Whatever you want them to do should be written as big and bold as your attention grabber.

On leaflets, there is no point of logos, no point in explaining how big your company is or how long you've been going – your viewer doesn't care about you, they care about what you can do for them.

Once you've got your text sorted, and you've decided on light centre or a border then you can start worrying about 'how pretty' you want to make it. There's a company called Smart Property Leaflets and if you go onto their website they'll send you 50 samples of property leaflets. They've been in the game a while and know what they're doing – check them out and decide for yourself.

Text, border (or light centre), layout – all checked and done. Now which weight works best? I'm asked this a lot and in my opinion 80gm leaflets are horrid, used by Taxi firms and 'low value' product companies. They don't take ink well, which means you'll get a lot of 'bleed' and slightly blurry text and they crumple up going through a letterbox.

You may get them cheap but, for BMV patches, they aren't up to the job of delivering your message. Your leaflet guys will bring back (or dump) hundreds of the ones that crease up too.

In my view there are two choices – 130gm or 170gm. 130gm will be cheaper and will suit most out there. They do crumple a little but, only through the stiffest of letterboxes. I use 170gm because I'm a bit posh, 170gm leaflets seem to go through most doors with one lengthways fold without creasing up – that suits my slightly autistic mind but, as everything, decide for yourself.

Glossy or matt? I'd never given it a second thought on which until I kept getting asked so instead of sitting on the fence I'd thought I'd give opinion.

If I asked you if the last Tesco leaflet that came through your door was glossy or matt could you tell me? Some will but, I suspect most of you wouldn't be able to and just make a guess.

In bright sunlight (unusual in the UK, I know) the light can bounce off a glossy on the floor and render the attention grabber unreadable therefore making your leaflet useless. And so, I have always chosen matt.

There isn't a wrong answer and I'm sure some will have an argument for the glossy but, as most won't be able to tell me about their others leaflets that land, I'm guessing that I'm going into too much detail here.

Once you've chosen an area of say, 4,000 houses in terraced streets not too far from where you're based. Let's split that area into quarters and manage each quarter week by week.

Each quarter contains 1,000 houses and delivering leaflets to those will be around a day's work. If you meet your new recruit on patch and hand over 1,000 leaflets, a door chart, an ice scraper, a pen you'll be on the way to getting your leaflets delivered.

I think that people like to be caught doing things right and that's why I'd recommended meeting them at around 10.30am wherever they're likely to be at that point. Usually, one third of their way round their route.

If you sit on a garden wall of a street opposite the street that they are working along, you'll be able to see them working, sometimes for the whole length of a street. When they reach you, go to meet them with a Snickers bar (other bars are available) and a bottle of water. Heaps of praise for a job well done and have a break together.

Doing this means that you've caught them doing something right, and likely you'll get a good delivery for the rest of the day.

This is the kindest way of managing leaflet staff but, there are others like GPS trackers and the like. These are not a way that I favour; I prefer the hands on personal approach. However, you should ask your leaflet guys to mark down any houses that are for sale on their route as that will tell you that they've been along the street and which houses to target on your three letter campaign (more on that later).

Lease Option Patch
If you are 'going after' Lease Option deals, you're leaflets may be entirely different and this is going to sound a little odd to get your head round to start with but I'll persevere.

I've found that the guys that live in the poorer areas that topple over in (financial terms) like a well-produced leaflet from a company that looks like they care, a professional outfit, hence my detailed explanation previously.

You'll get more lease option deals in slightly more affluent areas, those with middle managers, semi-detached housing, grass lawns, caravans, and two cars on the driveway.

I don't mean where the doctors and dentists live – leave them well alone for the time being but, just pleasant estates. I'll explain why.

The guys that live here are slightly more 'savvy' – they can take something a little creative. They are less likely to be behind on their mortgages. They'll have debts just as most of us do but they'll manage them better and have more to lose.

Putting a well-produced, professional leaflet in these houses doesn't always produce the results that I think it should.

Put an ugly leaflet through the door and you'll get tons – why? I'll try and explain. In business, we all like dealing with those that are less smart than ourselves, maybe we can get a better deal with them, and maybe they won't be able to scam me?

A hand written, badly spelled, scruffy leaflet can give the impression that you're just that little bit thicker and more desperate to do a deal – therefore, more likely to be easier to deal with than a corporate.

I realise that the above won't sit well with a lot of my readers but I'm just writing as I find in reality, not trying to tell you what you want to read. Your decision to go with what you're comfortable with, I'm not here to convince you.

TASK

Make up a leaflet, to start with a home printer, some canary yellow paper and word. You can set up three leaflets per page; they'll just follow the AIDA model.

Once you've made a template for your leaflet and got them printed, go out and deliver them to your patch. 1,000 leaflets will take a good days work of walking around.

The point isn't just to you to deliver leaflets but, also to get you 'walk your patch'

You'll discover more by 'walking your patch' than any internet research or reports. Talk to the people on the street, other *leafleters*, delivery people, window cleaners, odd job men.

Your day of delivering will be more fruitful than you expect. I've recruited delivery guys, got leads and made some discoveries about my patches that I might never have spotted sitting in front of the computer in my office.

The task is to get known by people in the area, you'll come across businesses that might display your leaflet for free, people on the ground know their area and often know who's struggling financially. They will have seen a car get repossessed at number 53; they'll know where their neighbours are buying their white goods.

The John Lewis delivery vans are quite distinctive and probably the indication that a family is doing well. The Brighthouse delivery vans are also distinctive and indicate someone paying over the odds for their white goods because they can't get regular credit.

If you spot a Cash Converters (or any pawn shop) pop in and have a look at the stock they're holding. All of the stock in these stores came from the neighbourhood. If it's full of fitness machines, that's not a struggling neighbourhood, if it's full of watches, gold jewellery, cameras, computers that could be an indication of people selling (or pawning) their valuables in times of need.

Let me know how your delivery day goes, I can guarantee that it will surprise you

2.3.5 Three Letter Campaigns

As well as being a way of checking the your leaflets guys have actually been up and down the streets you've issued them, this is another costs effective way of getting leads.

This type of campaign is simple in explanation but can be administration heavy unless you've got your systems in place. It's been around for years and I think it originally came from an American called Robert Allen. Anyway, I'll explain how it works.

Whilst your guys are out there leafleting, they'll come across properties that are for sale and have an estate agents board in the garden. These are the prospects for a three letter campaign.

Your guys can make a note of them on their rounds (full addresses) and you can target them for the campaign. On a recent course, it was advised to type the letters but hand write the envelopes as most people will open a hand written envelope when they get the post – I haven't done that in the past but, it seems like good advice.

Letter One

Congratulates the prospect on choosing the best estate agent in town and recommend a great removal company (do the research first). It then goes on to say that should the sale fall through, by all means give you a call to see if you can do something to help.

Letter Two

This letter is sent a couple of weeks later and congratulates the owner on the sale of their home (whether it has sold or not) and gives another recommendation of a great cleaning company. Again, the letter goes on to say, should the sale fall through, get in touch with you.

Letter Three

This letter is sent a couple of weeks after that again congratulating the owner on their sale and recommends a couple of websites with hints and tips of who to inform when moving house. Should the sale fall through, you are available to help...

The templates for the three letter campaign are on the website to download as word documents. The language and the way that they are worded are fairly important so it's worth the effort. Remember to have some systems set up before starting a campaign of this type as it's spread over a few weeks.

2.3.6 Newspaper Advertising

When dealing with those wonderful 'classified' sales people, it's often frustrating. They promise that your ad will appear on the right hand facing page of the newspaper (first place people tend to look at) when, in reality, they have no control on layout, editorial has control so, no matter what they say on the phone when collecting your card details. Often, and this is the frustrating part, is that they'll promise again and again giving away free inserts to compensate when you complain.

Let's deal with this in a slightly different way and save some of the frustration. Accept that you have little or no control where you're small advert is going to appear, once you're over that hurdle, you can work with what you have.

There are a myriad of opinions on advertising but, the only one that counts on your patch, is yours..!

You may make some mistakes here but, make them small – try an advert 2cmx2cm in plain text with a simple, dark border. Choose the newspaper that you think has the most readership. If you speak with any newspaper, theirs is always the most read. Make up your own decisions about the locals in your area.

There are free newspapers and 'paid for' – the choice is yours in which to advertise and there is no right answer on this. If you were making a blind choice then go for the paid as the 'frees' often get put in the magazine en route to the bin the following week. At least the 'paids' have a chance of being read by the purchaser.

This choice only works for an initial 'blind test' though. It should not be considered an absolute. Different areas have better 'frees' than 'paids' so check out who's reading what, which has the best reputation, which one has the better editorial. In short, make a decision based on 'your' facts and 'your' research not anyone else's.

Start small and with the smallest they'll let you. Grow from there and once it starts working and bringing in leads – always keep in the back of your mind that the only point of advertising is to bring in leads. If your paid advertising doesn't bring in leads, it's not working for you in this patch.

2.3.7 Bandit Boards

This strategy is one of my favourites although it's not risk free and certainly not 'hands off'. Have you ever driven past a lay by at 60mph and spotted a sign for 'flowers' only to have driven past it before you realised what it said or could do anything about it..?

This is the feeling that I get when I see most bandit boards out there, if only they'd taken the trouble to walk 200m further down the road, the response would have been 100% better.

There's two types of bandit board – pedestrian and road.

Pedestrian boards shouldn't be used for this strategy, in fact please don't put any boards up in residential areas, the neighbours will complain, the council will fine you and you'll get yourself into all sorts of trouble.

Just because your board has managed to stay in place, doesn't mean it's safe and working. People on the street will rip them down, paint over them, vandalise them. It's not worth the hassle of pedestrian boards in my opinion.

Roads boards, on the other hand, are an excellent way of getting leads that doesn't break the bank. You still have to check out how your local council deals with boards though. Better to be safe than sorry.

Road boards are those that are tied to lamp posts in 40mph zones, industrial areas, vacant commercial buildings and the like. It's a must to drive round your 'patch' to find out where the sweet spots are.

Let's deal with the message and font first – the message should follow the standard rules of advertising, AIDA – Attention, Interest, Desire and Action.

Someone has already done the 'font' research for us, and has been putting up signs for many years all around us. Why try and reinvent the wheel? The Highways Agency has figured out which font and size should be used to attract a motorist's attention.

When a speed limit changes (on the highway) there's a sign, usually quite a big one, and this is followed by three repeater signs that are smaller. It's those repeater signs that should interest you as this is the font and size that the Highways

Agency have deemed the minimum for a motorist to see at the required speed.

It wouldn't be a surprise to learn that they've put them at a researched height too. Stick with that which has been done before and copy. Same font, sized and height already works.

When driving around looking for sites, pay careful attention to 'sign noise' if you put up signs where there are loads of signs together, the chances of attention being paid to yours will be slim. You will be looking lamp posts with very little around them or 'lots of air' to make them as clear as possible to passing motorists.

The material to get them from is called Correx and is also used for Estate Agent and Letting Agent boards; it's common, inexpensive and readily available from most printers. Correx board does come in different colours but, printer's often just stock white board and print on sticky vinyl to make the message.

Prices vary from city to city but, if you venture into a high street printer expect to pay a fortune. You'll be looking for those little, back street printers with no shop front or retail presence. Often, these guys either trade online or supply online websites so there is no need for glossy shop fronts. This usually means the price will be significantly less.

In 2013, we are paying £10 (including VAT) per board, fully printed at 600mmx900mm.

The kit needed to mount boards isn't expensive either and most you'll already have at home. A pair of pliers, a stool (around 30cm high) with single legs so that it will balance and be sturdy on grass verges and a Stanley knife for cutting holes and cable ties. Not the cable ties from a supermarket, the good quality, thick ties (10mm) from a trade supplier. These will hold your board in place for longer but, don't put them up in temperatures below freezing as they have a tendency to become brittle and snap easily.

You'll be putting boards up in three's – the first board is the 'attention grabber' and it does not matter what this board says – could even be blank. Don't expect anyone to take anything from the first board at 40mph; its purpose is to move the motorist's vision in the direction of your message.

The next board is the 'Interest, Desire' board and should have your message on in print. Hand written road boards are not suitable for this strategy. Lay out your message clearly with good gaps (so the cable ties don't interfere with the letters).

The last board (lamp post three) is the call to action board – this board has a repeat of the benefits on the Interest/Desire board but also has a call to action. Mobile numbers are too long (and all different) to remember. This should be a short text code as they are easy to remember for a motorist that may drive past.

There are many 'short text' code providers out and to find one simply type the words 'short text code' into Google – you may even find one free that will also pay you revenue from each text.

2.3.8 Cars & Trucks

Sign writing anything big and in plain sight is desirable to get the most 'views' for your message. The advertising boards are expensive so the next best thing for you could be trucks. As with bandit boards, this is not a 'hands off' strategy as you will have to buy the trucks, maintain them, move them around, repair.

Cars and small vans from independent trade's people offer a slightly more 'hands off' approach to vehicle marketing. Reverse tack stickers are not expensive and can remain 'new looking' behind glass for many months.

Try asking some of the local trade's people on your patch if they'd mind having your message on their vans. Offer them something to compensate them naturally, a year's insurance perhaps...

I've found that 'Godiva' cars work just fine and they don't take a lot of maintenance but make your own mind up about how 'hands on' you wish to be.

Godiva cars (cars solely for advertising) are fully legal ie. Insured and taxed. They are parked in strategic places on your patch. They don't have to be on busy junctions but they do have to be visible to enhance your message.

2.3.9 Banners

What do I mean by banners..? Well, banners are the great big vinyl signs often seen on bridges, buildings and other structures purely for advertising.

They are usually made with reinforced holes at the edges so they can be attached with bungee cord or rope.

For this strategy to be successful, you're going to have to get out of the house and drive round your patch to find the spots that will get some traffic.

Please don't put banners across one of your properties or in residential areas, they'll annoy the neighbours and the council and cause you nothing but grief.

If you really must do these without permission, then have a look for empty commercial buildings close to high traffic areas like supermarkets and busy roads.

If you contact the commercial agent, they may allow you to site your banner on their security fencing for a fee. It only takes a phone call and they may be more accommodating than you think.

Banners are not expensive to produce, so if you have a spot in mind – pick up the phone and see if you can get permission.

2.4 Paper Shoots

This section has been written by Suzanne Bates, her company, Smart Property Leaflets has been producing leaflets for years. She can send over templates to choose from and have them printed for you. Suzanne is also an investor in the Midlands.

2.4.1 Designing Leaflets

What makes a leaflet 'good'? What's going to make people stop and read your flyer when it comes through the door instead of throwing it in the bin along with all the others that come with it? It may not be something they're actively looking for at that time but if it grabs their attention they will at least read it, and, if it then provokes interest or looks like a solution to a problem they will pick up the 'phone and call you. It may not be immediately, I've had people call me 6-9 months after they received the leaflet!

The Headline

This is THE most important part of any marketing information. Get it wrong and you've lost the prospective customer immediately. The best headlines appeal to the reader's self-interest, what's in it for them? A lot of inexperienced marketers make the mistake of using their business name as the headline;

'John Smith & Co', which, unless you are a well-known household brand name like 'Nike' or 'Tesco' is a complete waste of time as it doesn't mean anything to anyone!

The headline is critically important; it must grab your customers ATTENTION. Make it BOLD and LARGE so that it stands out. A good tip is to ask a question ie; 'Do You Want to Sell Your Property Quickly?' as people are naturally curious and will want to read on to find out the answer or how you can help to solve their problem.

What Size Leaflet Should You Use?

The size or the thickness of the leaflet isn't as important as what it says. A5 always works well (approx. 15cm x 21cm) as there is enough room to get all the necessary information on, they're cheap to get printed and don't weigh as much as A4 so they're quicker and easier to deliver too.

How Much Content Should You Add?

Remember KISS! Keep It Simple Stupid! No one wants to be bombarded with endless lines of text, no matter how relevant it may be. It looks and sounds boring. If you must include a lot of text, break it up into small paragraphs that are easy to read.

Write text as if you are personally speaking to a person and read it back to yourself aloud to see if it 'sounds' right, or ask someone else their opinion.

Benefits Sell - State the main benefits that the reader will get if he/she calls your company. Put yourself in their shoes and think about what they want to hear if they're looking to sell their property quickly due to mounting debts.

People have a tendency to 'scan' a page looking for the bits of information that are relevant to them (I bet you're doing that now!) so the best way to present your case is with the relevant bits shown in bold bullet points ie;

- **House Been On the Market for Too Long?**
- **Worried About Repossession?**
- **Need To Sell To Release Equity?**
- **Emigrating or Relocating?**
- **Debt Problems?**

'FREE' is a great word to use! People always want something for nothing, so offer to give something away

- **Free, No Obligation Consultation with Property Expert**
- **Free Confidential Advice**
- **Free Property Valuation**
- **Your Legal Fees Paid In Full**

Use Images

Images tell a story far better than words ever can, people focus on images before text. Pictures provoke thought so use them to your advantage :-)

Psychology plays a big part in marketing, so use pictures that make people relate to an emotion, like a house with a 'Sold' sign and a 'happy couple' (happy because they just sold their property) people will imagine their own house being sold.

You can even use pictures that promote bad feelings, like a photo of rows of properties with Estate Agent boards outside, drawing attention to the thousands of people trying to sell their property right now and how difficult it is. If the person reading it has their property on the market they will be forced to think about how long their own property may take to sell with an Estate Agent.

Testimonials
Testimonials are vital because they promote trust in you and your company. Testimonials with photographs of 'happy looking' people work even better because again it's a visual image that people will relate to. Ensure that the people in the photograph are looking directly into the camera as it's been researched that this type of photograph seems to be more genuine, and again, promotes trust.

Call to Action
Your leaflet MUST contain clear and concise 'Call to Action' information. It's no good saying 'if interested call 088000'. That sounds very feeble, like a lot of people won't be interested!

Make your call to action BOLD and easy to find. It's best to put it at the bottom and to the right of your leaflet as it's been shown that that's where people expect it to be, and use a female contact name if possible as it's been researched that people prefer to speak with a female. Having a picture of a smiling woman with the contact information can help.

If you can use a photo of yourself (or your partner) then this works well as the person the seller is contacting is seen to be more 'real'. People are naturally suspicious of anything that's unfamiliar to them so this makes you look more 'real' and promotes trust :)

0800 or Landline?

A lot of advertisers still use 0800 numbers as it can be advantageous to state 'FREE from land line' on your advert, but nowadays almost everyone has a mobile phone and therefore prefer to call another mobile or a local number, as it's costly to dial an 0800 number from a mobile. State on your leaflet that you're a 'Local Company', callers prefer it if you're in the same area, again it promotes security and trust, it will be familiar to them and they'll feel you can be easily contacted.

Some people prefer to email but I don't put email addresses or websites on my leaflets as a lead sent online can easily be lost. The competition online is fierce, keep your offline leads offline. Use email once you have your lead.

Use Scarcity – How many times have you rushed to buy something when you think there is only a limited amount available? Ie; Tickets for your favourite band advertised as 'Buy Now, Few Remaining– First Come First Served' It can work well on your flyers too! You could say

Call Now For Your FREE report – How To Sell Your House In 14 Days (limited availability) You could either write your own short report or find one online and edit it to make it your own (don't copy it outright or you could find yourself in trouble!)

2.4.2   Leaflet Distribution

How many leaflets should you deliver and what is the general response rate?

Generally people tend to start with either 5000 or 10,000 leaflets. Please bear in mind that as your distribution is not specifically 'targeted' at people who may need your services the response rate can be as low as 1 in 1,000.

So a distribution of 10,000 leaflets will bring you around 8 to 12 calls, it's a numbers game, you could get less, you could get more, this is just the average response for this type of leaflet. But remember, even if you only find one motivated seller, it will certainly make your campaign worthwhile! Of course this figure can vary according to certain factors like;

The Time of Year: Don't expect a great response around 8 weeks during the summer holidays and a couple of weeks before Christmas for obvious reasons

The Competition: There may be other investors in your area distributing at the same time – Is your leaflet better than theirs?

What Are The Best Areas To Cover?
You should be fairly familiar with the immediate and surrounding area you live in, so it stands to reason that you know what types of properties there are as well as what types of people live there. So this is a good place to start!

If you're not familiar with how much properties are worth in your own area it's a good idea to familiarise yourself by browsing on property sites regularly to get a 'feel' for how much properties are actually selling for. You need to know your area well so you can spot a 'bargain'! Use these sites:

http://www.rightmove.co.uk/

http://www.nethouseprices.com/

http://www.zoopla.co.uk/

Identify Local Authority Areas
Properties in these areas are generally well sized, have bigger gardens, they rent well because people who were bought up in the area and are starting their own family like to stay near to family and friends. You can also get them at a very good price so the yield will be higher than on larger private properties (with the exception of multi-lets/HMO)

When delivering to private areas stick to the smaller properties (2 & 3 beds) in areas that you've identified with good rental potential. These smaller properties are more lucrative, and again, have better yields. You can still get good deals on larger, more expensive properties but you'll need larger discounts to make the deal 'stack' and to make a decent profit.

Currently (2012) investors are looking for a discount of at least 25% + (unless they're using a Lease Option) but if you're acting as a 'Property Finder' remember to factor in your own fee.

How to Find Reliable Distributors
You may want to try using regular mailing companies like 'Royal Mail' but in my own experience they work out a lot more expensive, and, are not always reliable. It's better to have your leaflets delivered on their own rather than inside a

local paper or with 4 or 5 other leaflets as people are more inclined to throw these away.

It's cheaper and more reliable to recruit your own distributors, so write an advert saying something like:

Wanted In [This] Area

Self Employed Leaflet Distributors

Preferably Car Owner

Hours to Suit

Good Bonus Paid!

Please Call [Name] On [07777******]

Place the ad in local shop windows or on your local 'Gumtree' (if you have one in your area, it's free) www.gumtree.co.uk (or any relevant website) and you'll be surprised at how many replies you get!

How much you pay the distributor will depend on which area of the country you're in, currently in the East Midlands I pay my distributors £40.00 per 1000 (2013) and a £500 bonus when we complete on a deal. There's no set rules, make it a 'win-win' situation for yourself and the distributor by building a good working relationship with them. Going the extra mile to ensure they're happy will ensure that they continue to trust and deliver for you.

2.4.3   Leaflet Hand Outs

If you have leaflets printed, there's nothing to stop you from standing somewhere with a crowd to hand them out.

I've done this a number of times and there's some essential preparation to go through before you do it.

Firstly, choose an event, it could be a football match, car boot sale, high street shopping precinct, in fact, anywhere where there are plenty of people for a concentrated period of time.

I'll run through a sporting event as these have the most people. Visit the ground the day before to choose where you'll be standing, and somewhere to park the car as these events get busy beforehand. The last thing you'll want is a car loaded with leaflets, a schedule booked in and nowhere to park.

When you get to the event ground, have a look at each entrance and then look back over your shoulder to see if you can spot a bottle neck. This is an area like a pedestrian crossing, thinner bit of pavement – anywhere where the incoming crowd will get slower and tighter – directly opposite will be your 'stand'

At sporting events you'll only have around 25 minutes as the crowd enters the venue, so you'll have to work fast.

You'll need a set of steps or a reset, for somewhere to park your leaflet stock and a bottle of water that's not in the flow of pedestrian traffic.

You'll have 500-1,000 leaflets in your hand, in the centre of the pavement opposite your bottle neck. Get ready, we're about to meet the crowds.

As people start to approach you, they'll be slow during the first five minutes, most will be bumbling as these are the early ones, give yourself this time for practice. Lick your finger and thumb, and take off one leaflet from your hand. Separate, remove, eyeball your target, take one step forward and hold your leaflet straight out – as close to the chest as you dare on your target.

This seems bold but, it's the most efficient way of getting your leaflets out there. If you're meek and mild, you spend the time holding onto your leaflets and no one will take them.

Be bold and brazen – for the shy, this may take some deep breaths.

If they refuse, that's fine too, move on to the next target. If someone has their hands full (programs, food etc.) don't make them trip over trying to take your leaflet, let them go, there's plenty more.

As I said earlier, you'll have around 25 minutes of good crowd activity before everyone has disappeared into the venue, and this seems to be the general rule for sporting events, music events, fairs, shows and most venue crowd events.

Not so, for high streets, shopping centres and train stations and different tactics will be required here.

Shopping Centres

These are privately owned and often manned with security, if you're going to attempt this, it would be wise to have a 'spotter' as security will catch up with you and ask you to leave.

It's not a strategy that I do myself or ask others to do as there's no way of telling how successful you'll be or any real way of measuring your results.

I can't say, hand on heart that it won't work for you because I've seen plenty doing this with some results. If you are bold as brass, give it a go and let me know how you get on.

The town centre shopping precincts would seem ideal but, they often don't have our target audience so the smaller ones with the lower quality shops work better.

There's little point handing out leaflets outside John Lewis…

Train Stations

There are two great times to do train stations, the rush hours at the start and end of each working day. You'll get a rush of around an hour, maybe an hour and a half of busy leafleting done during these times. As with sporting events earlier, pick your spot with somewhere to store your spare leaflets and set to work. You'll see two busy periods during your shift. The middle managers and go getters have to get into the office for 8am so they're leaving before 7am, then the regular workers have to be in for 9am so you'll see another rush of 8am commuters.

Train stations are slightly different to sporting events as most people carry something to work so their hands maybe full, and there's often less space to pick a target that at a bottle neck.

You'll find yourself moving around a little to get the best spot but, the same guidelines apply. Pick your target, eyeball, and hand out close to chest.

I should mention that a great beaming smile is crucial – a smile will get your leaflets into more hands – approx. three times more and if you manage to spill someone's coffee on them on their way to work, you haven't had a good shift.

High Streets

Town high streets can be good as the traffic is slower moving, an ideal place to have a practice before a sporting event or train station.

Just because the traffic is moving slower, the same guidelines apply. Picking targets, one step forward, hand out, close to chest as you dare and remember that big beaming smile.

If you try City Centre high streets you may well be moved on, even though there's nothing illegal about handing out flyers, some city centres seem hotter on moving flyers on than others. Manchester seems not to like it and neither does Plymouth but most towns are okay.

If someone 'official' asks you to move on, then do so with good grace, manners and a big smile. You don't need the argument at this stage.

Some city centres charge businesses for litter – again, if asked, then you have a litter control policy which consists of you walking around the area picking up those leaflets that may have been thrown on the ground. It's only right, and they are your leaflets after all.

A word of warning – if you call your local council and ask if it's okay to hand out flyers, nearly all will say no, without even checking their own rule book – sometimes, it's better to ask for forgiveness than permission.

TASK

Join an online property forum and talk to others, you'll learn a bucket load; you'll also get opinions that will mean nothing. It's worth noting here that like magazines, forums carry topics on different strategies. Whilst opinion and argument is welcomed, it's important not to stray from your path too much.

Nothing wrong with changing your mind or ideas but, focus is a good thing.

There's lots of good advice however and forum membership can keep you just that little bit safer than not when deciding who to work with.

There's usually no cost to membership, and currently the two heavy weights are Property Tribes run by Nick and Vanessa. Another forum that formed last year is BMV Deals & Discussions, it's a Facebook Group run by Owais Naveed and you'll often find me on there. Practising what I preach, huh..?

Don't be shy, say hello, it's really me and I don't bite...

Word of warning – there are obvious politics and already formed relationships on forums, so take some time getting to know the personalities before wading in with some strong opinions. Add some value, as I'm sure you'll have experiences and knowledge that can add value to a forum.

3 Treble Your Conversion Rate

3.1 The Trouble with Trebles

The only point of advertising (for any business) is to get the phone to ring, that's your chance to get the lead details. Advertising (unless you're a medium to large company) isn't about branding yourself at this point. Bearing that in mind, logos have no real place on our advertising, style hasn't really got a place either. The most important thing is the 'Call to Action' – what do you want your prospect to do..?

3.1.1 Phone Numbers, Text Marketing

We all tried the 0800 number thing during the 90's as a way of increasing calls and it worked for a while, although nowadays,

I'm not sure that anyone actually believes it's a free call anymore. 0800 numbers are more useful to those companies that are 'national' based or wish to appear so. I don't, I want to be the 'local guy' on the ground, in the area.

I use local numbers, not 0845 (another bizarre form of charging) but just a regular local number with a local code. This number is a shadow number and routed through one of the many PA service companies. It doesn't actually exist; the call is just transferred through it.

Do I want to take the call? Well, I could but, if you're anything like me, you may get tongue tied when answering a lead call. You may be doing something else, have no pen and paper or just not ready to take a call. This is why I'd suggest using a PA; they are not expensive and can charge per call (per lead). A PA isn't given the details of any deal you can do and won't understand the details of your business. The sole job of the PA is to take the lead details: name, address, contact number and that's it. Of course, there's a way of doing it and scripts are available in the store but, essentially, there's no more to it than that.

Now, you'll have a lead(s) which can be entered into your tracking system, more on that later. The script to give your PA is below

Taking the Lead
Script 1 – Taking the lead details from a prospect call

The script below is used when a 'lead' or 'prospect' from your advertising calls. Sometimes it's difficult to refrain from dropping into a 'haggle' on the phone when an initial call is received. This script will enable you to resist that.

The idea is that if you are taking the call personally, you need to be merely, the detail taker, hence the script. A usual telephone greeting to start with, then ask if it's okay to take down a few details.

A caller will usually agree and then the script questions can be asked in order. Remember, at this stage, we only want the lead details. Price, or offers shouldn't be discussed, that discussion can be done on script two or in the house.

These questions can outsourced to a PA to take us one step removed from the process and, as its non-technical, there's no need to employ qualified sales staff.

Remember – the lead can be lost if offers or numbers are discussed at this stage

Property Script:-
- Name...
- Number...
- Address (post code)...
- Type property (drop down)...
- Bedrooms (drop down)...
- Estimated current value £...
- Outstanding loan £...
- How quickly would you like to sell?

- Reason for sale...

3.1.2 Making the Appointment on the Telephone

Around 60% of our successful business comes over the phone and starts as an enquiry. It is up to us to make sure that the enquiry is dealt with professionally.

It is our duty to make the most of that phone call because our vendors want to deal with us! But why? Because they want something. So, why do they buy from us? They want to buy from us because people buy people, but what does that mean? People buy people means identification i.e. having the same interest or hobbies or something in common.

Ok, how do I gain identification on the phone with someone I don't know? By having and creating *a 'tele presence'*.

Tele presence

Be under no illusions here: Selling an appointment on the telephone is far harder than face to face selling and it always will be, in fact telesales is an art in itself. What we can do is be better at it. So, back to tele presence, how do I get one? Three things and they are:

- Identification
- RSVP
- Can do attitude

Identification

The quickest way to gain identification is by using someone's name as often as possible during a call.

RSVP - Rhythm, speed, volume, pitch.
It's not what you say; it's how you say it!

- Rhythm
  - Rhythm the energy level in your voice, have a conversation with a friend and calibrate that at a level of 5 on a scale of one to ten. Then have the same conversation but on a level 6 to 7.See how much enthusiasm is transmitted during the second conversation.
- Speed
  - The speed we speak is around 150 to 180 words per minute however a person can think at 400 to 500 words per minute. So, if you have anything to say it had better be interesting or your listener will be bored quickly.
- Volume
  - Volume is something that people struggle with on the telephone, let the microphone do the work and speak at your normal, comfortable volume of speech.
- Pitch
  - The pitch of your voice can be used effectively by raising it to emphasize important points.

Voice exercises
Um-hmm one

Try it as an exercise; the word one as spoken in your exercise is YOUR normal pitch and volume.

Dropping plosives

Plosives are the sound that forces air from the mouth, i.e. b, d, g, k, t. If you drop the plosive letters, language becomes difficult to understand and the speaker sounds unsophisticated and uneducated. Examples are:

- B - pro'ly for probably
- D - 'ol for old
- G - runnin' for running
- K - dar' for dark
- T - hones' for honest
- T - liddle for little

If you mean to say yes, then don't say yeah, yep, yup or uh-huh.

Cork exercise

Uncork the bottle, place it between your teeth and read a passage in a novel aloud, as clearly as possible. Now, remove the cork and repeat the passage and see how clearly it was read because we are thinking about how we are speaking and not just what we are saying.

It's not what you say; it's how you say it!

Script 2 – Making the Appointment or lead qualification form

The script below is used on the follow up call after lead details have been taken down. You can use as much or as little as necessary to gain the appointment to visit the vendor.

Remember, the only purpose of this call is to make an arrangement to visit. We won't be discussing numbers or offer at this stage. If we do, we can lose the deal.

This script will allow you to ascertain condition and some points of deal viability. Be aware of competition, always assume you have some but, don't mention them.

INTRODUCTION

- Hello, can I speak to Mr/Mrs/Miss ....please.
- My name is Mark; from ABC Properties.....thank you for calling/texting your details......
- My wife and I specialise in buying properties quickly, for cash.....
- We usually rent them out.......
- And we also work with a large investment group when we need to buy properties to sell....
- In fact there are a number of different OPTIONS we can make available, depending on what you want to do
- So....I'm really ringing to discuss how we can help you......and wondered if you could tell me a bit more about your situation please.......is now convenient ?

THE PROPERTY

- You say it's a ....
- When do you think it was built?
- And How long have you lived there
- And Have you got somewhere in mind to move to
- You say it's in .... condition...
- Eg...How old is kitchen. Bathroom
- When was decorating done
- Any other work you have done to it

- Own driveway
- Garage
- Houses near by
- Are you on a main road?
- Next door
- What type of area is it?

THE LAND/GARDEN

- How much
- What is the condition of the land?
- Planning permission/ development....
- Any one built houses in gardens...

ON THE MARKET

- Why NOT with an estate agent
- How long has it been on the market?
- With Estate agent (s)
- How many
- Where
- Have they given you any feedback for why it hasn't sold?
- In order to know how we can best help you.....we need to understand exactly what sort of position you are in .....So the next few questions are designed to help us look at it from your perspective:
- What are you trying to achieve from this sale and what would be the ideal outcome for you
- Reason for moving
- What do you think it's worth?
- How much mortgage do you have outstanding on the property
- Any other secured loans

THAT'S GREAT, THANK YOU VERY MUCH

> - Now I need a little time to speak with my investor partners, when would be a good time to pop over for a chat..?

You'll need a script to call potential vendors, and rather than reproduce one here in full, it is important that it is your own. A script will come across as a script unless you write it, in your own words in the way that you speak.

I can't stress this enough, as so many sales people use canned scripts that get the phone slammed down on them.

Think of the information that you'd like to gain from the prospect beforehand and start from there.

A 'normal' conversation of 15 minutes could be split up with 9 open questions and 6 closed questions. The answers that you receive from open questions are usually longer than one word. They reveal detail and a little more information than you asked for. They create conversation.

Open questions being the following:

- How
- What
- Where
- When
- Who

A few closed questions in your script will make a conversation flow a lot better, if you'd like help creating scripts, then pop along to one of my workshops. We'll do them together.

3.2 Parking on the Drive

3.2.1 Preparation & Planning

Okay, we've made an appointment to see the lead. There's some research to do before we visit, most of it can be done online. Rightmove, Nethouseprices, MousePrice, Hometrack all offer valuation tools with varying degrees of accuracy and if you're using them, you don't know your patch well enough in my opinion. If you know your patch, you'll know the ceiling prices on every street, the movers and shakers in the area, the property that sells quickly.

I do use the online portals for infomation and some checking but, I generally know a price beforehand. In a BMV patch, a two bed terrace will sell for £85k in good condition, slightly cheaper without central heating, even cheaper if it needs a *refurb*.

I'd suggest getting around your patch and learn the prices:

- 2 Bed Terrace – mid and end – good condition and refurb required – ceiling price on street
- 3 Bed Terrace – mid and end– good condition and refurb required– ceiling price on street
- 2 Bed Semi – good condition and refurb required– ceiling price on street
- 3 Bed Semi – good condition and refurb required– ceiling price on street

1 beds and 4 beds are hard to trade, and quite specialist. At this point, let's do the easy stuff. It will make your trading (and

life) a lot easier than trying to do a deal with obscure properties.

If your PA has taken down the property details, the preparation can be a doddle. Draw the title deeds from the Land Registry for £3 but, please make sure that you are on the actual, official site as there are a few 'agents' out there that will charge more. The title deeds will tell you some vital information such as: the names of the owners (both or all), the price they paid, the bank that financed them and any charges or interests in the property.

There's also a wonderful benefit in having the document printed – some of your leads will have never seen a title document. That can be quite powerful when sat with a vendor, as you could know more than them about their own property.

Next stop is a valuation site, use any that will give you an idea of value and print it in BIG type on the page when printed. You'll be using this later on in the house, of course, only use it if the value is slightly lower and to your advantage.

Check the rentals in the area too, after all, you'll want to know that your deal will stack as a BTL product if you're trading on or keeping.

In short, you have the value, the rental, and possibly the condition. The title deeds are drawn, you've got the value in writing (in big print) and you're ready to visit the vendor.

3.2.2 Kerbside Checks

Unfortunately, everyone that I speak with ends the preparation and planning there, all of the due diligence done and off to see the vendor.

In my view, it doesn't end there. Kerbside checks are done in every walk of professional life. They may be called something different but, they are really just the same.

Before I went on a mission as a soldier, we'd check the ammo, we'd check the weapons, we'd check the strength of the radio batteries, we'd pack and repack our kit.

We did the checks, because if our kit messed up during a mission, it could be the difference between life and death so they were quite important to us as individuals and as part of a team.

As a soldier, we'd use the 'buddy buddy' system which meant that, as soon as my own kit was checked, I'd check my buddy's for him and vice versa.

In corporate life, before a call we'd check our briefcases, our paperwork and so kerbside checks are vital to a good vendor visit.

A vendor visit may not mean the difference between life and death but, you're doing this to make money right..? It can make the difference between deal and no deal.

Probably, the last thing to remove from the briefcase is the self-evaluation form and put it on the passenger seat of the car. This is to remind you to complete it as soon as you leave the call. It's the only time you'll be honest with yourself. If you don't get the deal and arrive home you'll start to make things up in your head – we all do it. The fault for not getting the deal will become the vendors, they were too stuck on selling, their price was too high, or wanted to move too fast. As you begin to visit vendors, you see the same objections time and time again but, until you admit to yourself that you have to get over them, you'll blame the vendor.

I'll say that again, because it's important – put the self-evaluation form on the passenger seat of the car before you go in the house. If we eventually do some coaching with you, this is one of the tools we'll use.

3.2.3 The 5%'s – The Devil is in the Detail

The 5%'s are those little personal details that make the difference between someone with a great conversion ratio and someone that hasn't. Each 5% individually won't lose you a deal but, if I meet someone that isn't doing well, I'll guarantee there's a few of them missing. You may think these are superficial, they add up to the whole presentation to your customer.

I'll give an example here – not brushing your hair won't lose you a deal (perhaps) but, a few of the 5%'s will show. The 5%'s seem simple but, they make the difference, the devil is in the detail as they say. Your customer may forgive the odd 5% but not a few of them.

So, what are they? It's the personal grooming, the time keeping, the tidiness and order of their paperwork, the car they drive. The way you handle your paperwork, your calculator, nerves will show if you haven't practiced.

Please don't turn up to a vendor's house in your, We Buy Houses Fast, signed up Luton van, as you'll be asking for trouble and no deal. Vendors have all sorts of reasons for wanting discretion, the neighbours' curtains twitching, a nosy family member; or they may just be private people. Your Luton van will be anything but discreet and may cost you the deal.

Going the other way can be just as bad, if you show up to a vendor's house in your new Bentley, expect to be shown the door pretty rapidly. Of course, they won't say it in those words; they'll waste a couple of hours of your time first.

Your dress is one of the 5% too – dress in jeans and a tee shirt and your 'rapport-building' to the over 40's has just gone out of the window. Some course you attended may have told you to dress casually but, in reality, you'll be insulting most of the older generation that you meet. If you can't make an effort, they won't do business with you.

Of course, there are exceptions to prove the rule – someone you'll meet at a networking meeting will tell that they always go to see vendors in their scruffiest jeans because, 'they're just a bloke' and it may work for them. For most of you, especially, if you're starting out and you're in your mid-twenties, with a vendor in their forties, you've got enough rapport-building work to do without putting nails in your own coffin before you even get in the house.

Again, there's a balance – going the other way can be just as bad. The fitted suit, pocket handkerchief, braces, pointy shoes and oversized watch will have the same effect but, in a different way. You'll become a 'suit' and 'suits' are to be untrusted, the uphill battle just got steeper.

Smart casual is an odd term but, it's the best way to describe the way to dress for a vendor visit – vendors aren't business people so leave the suit at home but, we can all tell when someone's made an effort or not. Make an effort…

Things to check we have with us:

The title deeds to the property, our sales comparables, our option agreement, an option contract (sample), an exchange contract (sample), testimonials from previous customers.

3.3 Sitting on the Floor

3.3.1 Appointments

When making an appointment, it's usual to make appointments for an evening, just because you'll catch most vendors in together. You need to see all owners on the title deeds, if you don't you'll be wasting a lot of time on second visits and as a result deals falling over.

I'd suggest making appointments at specific times so you are running your own diary. I realise that you may be enthusiastic and want to see everyone as soon as possible but, you could end up working hard but, not smart, if you let others run your diary for you.

I see vendors on Monday-Thursday evenings and one call on a Sunday morning. Friday's are difficult to catch both in, and no one will want to see you on a Saturday evening.

Okay, you're in the house, and it's time to figure out how to play the 'sit' – I often go where I'm directed by the vendor and you may have to as well. If I had a choice, I'd go for the living room. It's where you'll build the best rapport, and it's their 'place' in the family home to discuss important things that will affect their future life. Remember that vendors are not business people, so sitting with them in the living room is the softest approach.

I've said the same thing for years to start the 'sit' and my introduction is below:

"I've no idea whether we can do any business or not at this stage but, have you any objections to a few questions regarding your circumstances and your property?"

You'll have to come up with your own introduction (or copy mine) but, the important thing is to ask permission to ask some questions. Once you've been given permission, you can ask as many as you like.

3.3.2 Introducing yourself
To ensure the structure of the meeting is "action producing".

Action is only ever the result of motivation. If someone acts, something at some stage motivated them to act so vendor visit should always obey the rules of motivation, which is a two-step process

- Step 1: FIND OUT what the vendor wants
- Step 2: SHOW HOW he can get what he wants with our product

These two steps represent the basic structure of any persuasive process. DESIRE: Building desire is often talked about. Salespeople are usually aware of its importance, but are usually unsure exactly how to go about it. It is useful to look at building desire through the eyes of the above two steps.

- Step 1: We find out what the prospect wants. We build the importance in his mind of the value, the benefit of what he wants.

- Step 2: We then show how our product does what he wants, how it matches his requirement. This translates desire for a solution into desire for OUR solution. So: Matching builds desire.

3.3.3 Going Against Competition

Whenever possible, never mention your competitors by name because it's free advertising and it raises the prospect's confidence in your competitors, so don't always assume that you are up against competition. You might be or you might not be. Business is often lost because the vendor is too aware of the competition and consequently inadvertently suggests it to his prospect with the phrase:

- "Are you seeing anybody else?"

It's unwise to use this phrase as the prospect could think "Maybe I should!" Instead, try these alternatives:

- "Have you done anything about this so far?"

OR

- "How far have you got with this?"

OR

- "What plans have you got for solving this situation?"

Wherever possible don't talk about your competitors at all.

If you must talk about them:

- Don't call them "Our competitors"
- Don't say "The competition"
- Don't say, "Compared with us"

All these phrases simply add credibility to the strength of your so-called competition.

Don't knock your competitors. Knocking is unprofessional and most people regard it as such. It also breaks the basic rule of business

- What you hand out, you get back.

Establish your unique sales points (USP's). Selling against competition is all about selling the difference. Take your product out of competition by accentuating the difference. Build desire for the difference.

3.3.4 Signpost

What is a signpost? Our lives are signposted, road signs, restaurant menus, book contents, even a clock is a signpost.

At the beginning of any meeting in business there's an agenda, that's a signpost. If someone uses that agenda to give their audience a run through of what's about to happen, they'll take the audience along with them. Giving a great signpost is the key to the start of a great meeting.

Now you're all sat comfortably and you've gained permission to ask a few questions, a signpost is exactly as it's suggests. You'll be giving directions on how you'll conduct the meeting.

I was once in a business meeting with the senior management team in a previous life. The cars in the car park were enough to suggest that this would be a direction changing meeting. I grabbed a coffee and sat at one corner of the huge, dark wood table.

Everyone started to come into the room with their coffees and chose a place to sit. I could feel the tension in the room, and could tell by everyone's posture that everyone else could too.

The lady hosting the meeting was called Helen; she was the new HR director. Helen stood up, which is unusual in business meetings, she started her introduction.

She guided us through an introduction, and what the HR plans would be for the company for the coming year, and how her team was going to help us on the ground. Helen then went on to describe how she was going to re-arrange her team so it could serve us better.

During the meeting she would be letting us know how we could give feedback to her and her team so that they could keep on track and improve during the year.

Helen had only been with the business for 6 days, and this was her first meeting. She had us all glued to our seats for over 12 minutes with her signpost. Because she gave a great signpost, she held the room for an hour and a half. If your signpost is good, you'll hold the room with your vendors for enough time to make the deal work.

Sometimes, my signpost does the job so well, that the vendor will ask where we are on my agenda... That's an indication, that you gave a great signpost.

Let the vendors know where you'll be going. The headlines on this chapter are a good signpost, if you let them know where you'll be going, they come along with you.

3.3.5 Fact Find

This section of the meeting is the most important part and I would suggest some further reading at this point. There's a chap called Neil Rackham who worked for IBM during the eighties. Neil wrote a book called, the SPIN Selling Fieldbook. He takes a journey of the 'fact find' phase of a meeting in intricate detail. In my opinion, his book is worth its weight in gold.

Neil Rackham, in his book, shows how classic sales techniques such as closing and objection-handling can actually reduce your chance of selling, especially in sales situations where a possible life changing decision is being made.

Overall, the method, like many other approaches, is a 'hurt and rescue' approach. You find their problem and 'hurt' them by exposing the terrible things that might happen (spot the use of tension). Then you rescue them with your product.

The four question types are described below. There's much more detail of the sequence in the original book.

Situation questions

In important sales, minimize the small talk and focus on finding background detail that can be used to make sense of the vendor's situation. Context creates meaning. This is about understanding the wider context before you zoom into the details.

Problem questions

Ask questions to uncover problems which you can address. If you were selling tractors, you'd ask about maintenance costs, breakdowns and so on. If you were selling life insurance, you'd ask about how many dependents the person has.

A trap here is to dive straight into presenting the benefits of what you are selling. You may know the problem, but they do not! Going straight to the sales pitch will just get you objections.

Implication questions

Instead of telling them the problem they have (which is also likely to raise objections), the goal is now to enable them to see (and feel!) the problem. By asking questions, which draw out the implications of the problem, they get to feel the pain that will drive them towards your product. This is the 'hurt' of Hurt and Rescue.

For example, the person selling tractors might ask about implications of unploughed fields, whilst the life insurance salesperson could carefully ask what would happen to the children if the target person died or became very ill.

Need-Payoff questions

Having 'hurt' the target person with your implications, you now give them a straw to grasp at by asking how their pain could be resolved. With careful questions, you can get them to the state where they are asking for your product even before you show it to them. This is a very neat 'rescue' of Hurt and Rescue, where they either rescue themselves or ask you to rescue them.

For example, the tractor sales person can ask how much better the tractor was when it was new, or whether any of the farmer's neighbours have solved problems of old and problematic tractors. The insurance sales person could ask questions that build pictures of the target person's children being safe and secure whatever curve-balls the world might throw at the family.

3.3.6   List of Questions
Below is a list of questions within each of these categories plus some initial rapport building questions.

These questions within each section are not in any particular order – that is so that you don't blindly follow the list, but use your own skills in obtaining the information that you require.

Also, your aim is to have a directed conversation with the vendor whereby you get the information that you require and the vendor gains the confidence to sell their property to you. So, if they answer a question and give some useful additional information, take their lead and follow it. For example:

You: So, when are you hoping to sell?

Vendor: As quickly as possible because I'm now behind in the mortgage payments and my credit card company has just started sending me red letters..

You: How behind are you in your payments on both the mortgage and credit card?

Rapport Building Questions (examples)
- Hi I'm "X" could I take your name please?
- What accent is that?
- How was work today?
- How do you pronounce your surname?
- How can we help you?

Problem Questions (examples)
- What other challenges / problems might you be facing at the moment?
- I know you have reasons for saying that do you mind me asking what they are?
- How long do you think it would take to sell on the open market?

Need / Pay Off Questions(examples)
- What would be your perfect outcome?
- What time frame would you like to complete by?
- Would selling by the end of this month suit you?

The questions are not in a chronological order, they don't all have to be asked and they certainly shouldn't be scripted – they are just to stop that awkward silence if you run out.

3.3.7 Critical Time

By the end of your fact find phase, you'll have a pretty good idea if there's a deal here or not and critical time is your chance to carry on with the meeting or politely exit.

There's an argument to suggest that you could stay just for practice even if you don't want the deal and there's nothing wrong with practice. Be aware of your time and make some notes if you are not keeping the deal, self-evaluation is a crucial tool for improvement.

If you decide to exit, then do so with some grace. You'll likely know someone that could help the vendor, even if you don't want the deal. Let them you'll pass their details on, and, in return, now they know what you do, perhaps they know of someone that you could help.

'Exiting' gracefully will bring you more *leads* than you'd think. People always know someone else in a similar position, or will do in time.

3.3.8 Match

This is the phase of the meeting which will make or break the deal. There's a number of buying tools that you could have at your disposal and whilst they won't all be relevant, it's worth mentioning a few. If you don't know how to put together a deal using these buying tools, then please seek further training. I can recommend some, if you'd like.

On this section, I'll just be talking 'deals' ie. No carrying wood or bricks, no *refurbs* or upside down deals – just regular, simple stuff to keep or trade.

BMV Offer – In the old days, a tradeable deal had to stack at 25% BMV (Below Market Value) and cashflow at £250 (gross) per month on a single let AST (Assured Shorthold Tenancy). If you're keeping it, make your own judgement but, trading has a certain criteria. Not a golden rule, just a general rule to keep in mind.

These types of deals work when there is plenty of equity in the property and it suits the vendor.

Lease Option – This buying tool works when there is no equity but, the vendors existing mortgage allows the deal to cashflow. I'd suggest a term of no longer than 7 years on each deal but, the maximum permitted by law is 21 years.

Instalment Contract – This buying tool is used when the vendor would like the security of a sale as you'd be exchanging contracts with the vendor with an instalment contract. Sometimes these are called (EDC) Exchange with a Delayed Completion.

They are lots more but, to start with, you'll be concentrating on the basics to allow you to trade the deal on and these will all allow you to do that simply. Always seek legal advice and use trade lawyers to put the actual contracts together.

All you'll need in the house is a simple option agreement to secure the deal which is sent to your lawyer to draw up.

Building your offer from the Ground Up

Let's say that you've built a good bit of rapport by asking questions, actively listening, caring about the answers with your vendor. You're having a good visit so far. You may, at some point be invited to have a look around the property. I only ever look round when I'm invited, remember, you're in their turf now, follow their lead.

If I'm completely honest, I don't care too much about the house, I've seen thousands of Victorian mid terraces and they all begin to look the same but, there are a couple of tips on the *walkaround* that I'll share with you.

When I approach the house, just before the meeting, I look up at the roof, if the central roof line is straight and all of the slates are there, chances are that the roof will be fine however; it's not quite straight there could be some expensive remedial coming or go for a hefty discount to cover it.

My terraces always seem to have damp in two places. They are the front wall below a bay window and the single storey kitchen extension at the back. Other than those two places, mid-terraces have stood for a hundred years so they aren't likely to fall down the day after you complete.

When I visit the loo, I'll wash my hands and this will tell me what sort of boiler the property has without even looking. If the hot water comes on at full temperature fairly quickly and remains constant and hot, chances are they've got a fairly modern combi boiler (and it works) – anything other than this it may mean remedial work.

On our tour round, the light switches will give an indication of the age of the wiring, they vary slightly in colour and design every few years. The radiator style will also give a clue to the age of the heating system.

The kitchen is a prime area for a spot check – fitted kitchen carcasses last for ages, especially the 18mm ones so even if the doors are tatty, it may not be a lot to spruce up the kitchen.

The bathroom will be another area to check. I often find those wonderful turquoise bathroom suites with a cast iron bath and an electric shower over. This lot will be coming out and replacing, as it's not worth the risk – the vendor will have no idea of the age of the shower and if they do, they'll lie. It's funny how every single electric shower that I come across has been replaced in the last five years – I've never had one older. There must have been a sale on across the country in electric showers five years ago…not..!

As last checks – the fuse board (consumer unit) and boiler just to see if you can see evidence any upgrading or servicing will help you trade the deal later on so they are well worth the check. Look for servicing stickers from engineers or newly added circuits on consumer units.

Lastly, the windows. If I'm keeping the deal, I'll avoid wood windows on terraces with bays as they quite expensive to replace. If trading, it doesn't really matter as the expense isn't yours but, always look as you'll get asked the question at some point.

If they are double glazed, have a check of each pane to spot condensation. Individual pains are not expensive to replace but, you'd like to know many so you can budget.

Staining isn't important as there are some wonderful products in the caravan world that can bring up UPVC to its former glory. A bit of elbow grease and they'll look like new.

Just on refurbishment – I'll be getting a survey and professional advice if I'm keeping the deal. I'm not a surveyor and I won't be doing the work so I can't stress this enough – this book is about deals, not repairing properties. For refurbs, and all other 'hands on' jobs, obtain professional advice and get the guys in that know what they're talking about.

Having said all that, and completed the 'look round' I wasn't even looking for the condition, after all, I'm just after the deal so the work and condition is a little irrelevant. The real reason for the look round is to see if I can spot where they keep their paperwork. The bills, the final demands, the debt letters. Everyone keeps them somewhere, I've just got to find them.

I keep all of my financial files in one room; I call it the library, even though, in reality, it's just a 6'x6' room that we don't use for anything else. Anyway, vendors never seem to have a library or their files in one place. They keep them in all sort of strange places.

Some could be by the door, that's often the unopened debt chase letters; some could be in a magazine rack in the living room, some in the kitchen drawer. I even found paperwork under the bed, wherever it is, I have to find it because I'm going to use it later on in the visit to do the deal.

Once I think I've spotted their 'filing' system, I ask for the mortgage statement. This is that piece of paper we all get once a year with how much we've paid. Everyone gets one; nobody can ever find it but, when you've asked, keep your mouth shut. Don't say another word until you have it in your hand. Why? Because people come up with sorts of excuses and babble about where they last saw it, where they keep it, how they mopped up a split coffee with it, in fact, you'll often get a wonderful story from that one question if you ask it in the right place.

Once you have their 'spot' you can refer back to it later during your visit and even take all of the paperwork downstairs too.

If you don't get hold of the paperwork during the look round, you are going to have to ask for it. The reason being is that as humans we like to offer our thoughts, or give answers to questions, even when we don't know the answer – we'll even make it up on occasion, just for something to say.

If you don't believe me, ask any Policeman about how varied eye witness statements can be, from witnesses that saw the same incident you'd think they were in a different country at the time.

The point is, don't believe a word anyone tells you, you need the paperwork to work with facts – it's the only thing that counts during a visit.

I carry a file; it's actually a 40mm Lever Arch file from Staples, not as big and bulky as normal office lever arch files so it's handy. Mine has its own dividers already inside so when I start to go through their paperwork, I can file it straight into its own section to build a picture up of their financial status.

How is each monthly payment on each debt, who's chasing them, how many CCJ's – I'm not going to clear their debts for them or give any financial advice but, I am going to base my offer on what evidence I get from the files.

This paperwork is vital if you are going to use a debt management company to help them reduce their debts and bills to enable them a better quality of life too. At this point, I want a deal that works for them, not me. I don't believe in win/win at this point, I believe in win for the vendor. If it works for them, then maybe we'll do a deal. If it doesn't work for them, then I can't do a deal.

I won't question your ethics or morals on this; you can do that for yourself. I mentioned earlier that I've been blessed with a tremendous amount of energy, and I do lots of stuff. If you do the lead work properly and drag in loads of them, you'll be able to pick and choose who you work with. If you skimp on the lead work, you'll get 'deal desperation' – you'll try and make a silk purse out of a sow's ear, because it's all you've got with which to work.

Deal desperation isn't a nice place to be, and I know as I've been there – so avoid it like the plague.

I tend (and advise you too) not to work with the over 60's because, no matter how good a deal you do for them, their kids (if they have them) can come back to haunt you. Kids can get a little bit giddy where money's involved, especially if they think that you ran off with their inheritance.

Another group I tend not to deal with are those so close to repossession that I'd have to go to court. *Repos* are a specialist field and should be dealt with by those that do that kind of work. If you're new to sourcing deals, the last thing I'd advise doing is a court repo, you'll likely end up looking like a disorganised fool in front of a courtroom and a judge. Do this too early and you won't want to go back until you learnt what you're doing.

Don't get me wrong; it can be lucrative and great work but, get some training so you know what to expect. It will be a lot easier going into a judge for the first time if you know what you're doing, as opposed to visiting a second time after a first humiliation.

If you do come across *repos*, I can put you in touch with a couple of experts in their field.

Another group I tend not to deal with are the mentally challenged. These aren't a big group but, it's worth a mention just in case. It would be an easy deal perhaps but, I'd like to sleep at night knowing that I did the best thing I could and that I am ethically sound. Don't take advantage and you'll be in business for a long time to come.

Property lease options are a solution to some people's property dilemmas, but so many of these people are unaware of how they work and how they can offer another way to invest or sell a property.

There are lots of situations where people can't sell as the lending criteria continues to become increasingly stringent so their sales fall out of bed. Lenders can also move the goalposts without warning. This can also make it exceedingly difficult for first time buyers to own a property of their own.

The solution is to find a motivated seller who is unable to sell and is willing to give you time to build the deposit required by the lenders, this can be facilitated through legal paperwork with a property lease option – which is the option to buy in a few years' time.

In return for this opportunity the buyer puts down a small deposit, say 3-5% and make a monthly payment towards buying the place and agrees a fixed price and a timescale within in which to exercise the option to buy.

3.3.9 Pre-Close

To close the deal without the pressure, a pre close can be used to 'test the water' – a text book way of pre closing is:

- "If I could……would you…"

i.e. If I could satisfy all of your needs/wants, would you be able to make a decision tonight. If the response is negative, then simply go back to asking more questions. If the response is positive, then you can go ahead and close the deal.

3.3.10 Close
I've learnt through reading many books that closing is difficult, and I don't like difficult so I use the fastest and easiest way to close up a deal that I've found. Simply hold out your agreement and your pen and ask for a scribble. A signature is way too formal, and holding out the pen is the easiest way to ask someone to sign.

Do not speak whilst you're holding out the paper and pen, if you do, you'll lose the deal. This is often referred to as a silent close, arguably, the most powerful close in any situation.

How long do you stay silent? As long as it takes, the only person feeling any pressure will be you. It's natural for a person to think about your question, and their answer. There's no need to interrupt that thought process, so don't.

3.3.11 Objection Handling
There are lots of books written on objection handling and I'd say just one thing. If you get objections after you've closed, then you didn't do a good enough job through the previous phases. As long as you can admit that, then you can move on and do a better job next time.

The text book way of handling objections is to agree – with whatever the vendor says. The reason for doing this is because it will stop an argument with your vendor. It's incredibly difficult to argue with someone who's agreeing with you, although someone forgot to let my wife know that..!

We agree and we agree, no matter how daft the objection seems to you.

After we've agreed, we can use the **Feel, Felt, Found** process. This process has been around for years and sometimes it even works.

It goes something like this...

- I can understand why you feel like that..... (agreement)
- Some of my other customers felt like that to.....   (still agreeing)
- What we've found is that once they'd tried this solution, they found it worked for them.... (outweighed)

I'm certainly not going to tell that this process will work, it's not a magic formula and it will take some practice to master but, it may tip a deal your way if you use the process correctly.

3.4   Painting the Door

3.4.1   Consolidation

To help your deal 'stay in bed' this phase is crucial. After you've left the house, your vendor may have a friend round or visit the pub. They'll chat with their mate, 'Fred'.

Would you think their mate Fred is positive or negative about their transaction..? He sucks the air through his teeth, and gives a, "You didn't want to do that" comment that will throw doubt in your vendors mind.

Fred wasn't there during your 'sit' and he certainly doesn't know the details of your deal. It's easy for Fred to criticise as it's not him that's in the position of your vendor.

To stop this happening, consolidate your deal before you leave. It's a simple process but, it has saved me many deals.

Go through, in 'baby' steps, what's going to happen next – the valuer may visit, the lawyers may call or email. If you're dealing with a younger vendor it may be the first time that they've sold a property so show them an example of the contracts.

Give them confidence that you'll be with them every step of the way, and that you'll keep in touch throughout the process. This is even more vital if you're trading a deal as you'll have some of your timeframes dictated by your buyer and their lawyer's.

I come across more deals than I'd care to mention, that *fall over* because of poor consolidation.

In the appendices is a typical Option Agreement, and this is the piece of paper that secures you the deal, so do please review and adjust as required.

TASK

This task involves other people. Before you sit in a vendor's house and try a deal, it's important to practise. Practice takes away the 'ums' and 'aah' and 'erms' out of a meeting. It's one of those things that we all do when we're not confident in what we're saying.

Rehearsal is crucial and I'd advise carrying out at least ten before you sit in a live situation. Choose friends, family or any property people. Property people are probably the best for this as they'll understand what you're trying to achieve.

Let them ask questions too, because if they ask, it means they didn't understand – if they didn't, your prospect won't either.

Give your practice partner as real an idea as possible of a scenario beforehand and let him come up with his own answers as he will be drawing from personal experience and his own values – just like a real prospect would.

Remember, things don't always go how you think they should, people can say the strangest things. That's real life and it would be impossible to go through every answer in a book, that's why we practise.

If you practise with someone who's experienced in their field, it's called coaching and consider feedback to be all important and vital to your development.

3.5 Getting Creative

Buying tools are not strategies; they are tools that help you put a deal together. If someone says to me, I'm just after lease option deals; it just tells that they haven't got any money. Lease options aren't something to look for; they are just a tool to help the vendor sell their property.

So, to keep the confusion at bay, let's look at some tools and your route to market.

3.5.1 BMV offer
A straight, discounted offer from the market value. A tradable deal is typically 25% BMV with £250 gross monthly cashflow. These can be traded to other investors, or the retail market. The property is sold using the usual contracts.

3.5.2 Lease Option
An offer to 'babysit' the vendor's mortgage and buy at a later stage. A lease option is the right but, not the obligation to buy the property. Lease options can be traded to other investors or sold on the retail market to those that have had difficulty securing finance with the mainstream lenders.

3.5.3 Instalment Contract
These are similar to lease options but, the property is exchanged therefore the buyer is obligated to buy. These are sometimes seen as more secure for the vendor as the property has exchanged. Often called Exchange with a delayed completion. These are not usually traded with other investors

but, to consumers that have difficulty financing using the mainstream lenders.

An instalment contract is also referred to as *delayed completion* or *long stop*. It's a way of legally buying a property but delaying the time between exchange and completion. You enter into an agreement with the buyer or seller, whereby you commit to buy the property at an agreed timeframe. It's different to a property *lease option* where you can decide at the end of the term what you want to do with the property – this way you are legally required to complete the sale. It's essential that you get the right advice before entering into this agreement and are clear on the requirements and conditions of such an agreement. An *instalment contract* allows you to purchase a property without going through the traditional route and finding a hefty deposit in order to you to either start a property portfolio or buy a home for you and your family.

Why do people take out an instalment contract?

The reason that people delay the completion on a property will differ between properties, buyers and other interested parties. One common reason is that the property is in negative equity and an instalment option will give the seller and buyer (and everyone else involved!) time to switch to neutral equity, then afterwards positive equity making it a much better deal. Another example is that the seller wants to have their price, and is willing to wait. Another reason is that a property could be pending planning permission or that a submission to make the property an HMO is pending. It's a way of delaying what you can't do or what you want to do with the property today yet not losing out on selling or buying the property subject to these special terms.

There are other buying tools like *flips*, *assisted sales* and more but, for trading, I'd stick to the three main tools. There are organisations around who will be able to teach the other models if you need them.

When trading, you'll have to decide who your end buyer is so you can decide your exit strategy from the deal. The exit is as important as buying, as that's when your full profit is realised.

Each exit strategy comes with its own marketing streams which have to be put together. If your end buyer is an investor, then building your list of investors will your main task. If you decide your exit is a consumer, your marketing will be different.

Don't try and complicate things to start with so that any mistakes you make are small. Choose a route, focus on that route and become the best that you can be at that route.

3.5.4 More on Lease Options

If you are closing a lease option deal, there are a few tips here. Few vendors will like the idea of you controlling their property for an amount of time without you actually buying it so you may have to reassure them.

Lease Option agreements - Benefits to buyer and seller

A lease option is a very good agreement for both buyers and sellers. With the help of this contract, a house is sold over a period of time, usually at the current market value. In this case buyer (usually an investor) and seller, both benefit, creating a win-win situation. For a lease option to be successful it is critically important that the deal is meticulously drafted. While making a lease agreement it is better that you take help of a professional who knows all the clauses and rules and can draft the agreement.

Advantages of the lease option for the sellers

The major benefit is that those wishing to sell can lock in the property at a price at the market value even when there is slowness in the property market.

There is often little cost to selling a property using a lease option, the mortgage payments are taken over and the seller can walk away and start afresh. This is especially attractive in a slow property market.

When it comes to lease option, the seller is assured to attract the best quality clients with genuine interest in the house (usually an investor). Hence a lot of unnecessary enquiries are eliminated in the first place.

The buyers (the investor's clients) who opt for the 'rent to own option' always take better care of the house and property and are serious about the maintenance and up-keep. Thereby the current owner does not have to worry about the expense of repairs and is assured about the proper protection of his property until the lease option is exercised and the property sold.

With a proper contract and precise clauses in place the mentioned factors are covered and hence peace of mind for the seller is assured.

When the deal closes; there is no extra cost for the commissions to third parties.

The seller also gets to retain tax advantages of ownership until the time property is sold.

With proper structure in place the seller can get debt relief, even if the mortgage is higher than the market rate.

Furthermore, there is equity build up as the mortgage balance is reduced.

There are two sides to any leasing agreement, and you would do well to be benefitting both sides as best as it can. Due to so many advantages a lease option is one secure way to fulfil the dream of owning a property for a buyer. While the seller also gets to enjoy the situation, which provides equal opportunities, a balanced agreement is a good bet and very important for a positive final outcome.

Let's look at a particular deal from the seller perspective:

- Market value: £159,950
- Outstanding Mortgage: £112,000

The seller would like to move on with their lives, but the property isn't selling. A lease option can be drafted to offer the market value for xx years. The buyer (investor) takes over the mortgage payments for that period. At the contract end, the property is sold for the market value at that time, and any profit (above £159,950) goes to the investor. The seller enjoys a profit of £159,950 minus the original mortgage of £112,000 which equals £47,950. This profit comes back to the seller having made no mortgage payments for the period of the option. A valuation (or research) would normally be carried out on the property. The mortgage payments are the responsibility of the buyer (investor) who pays from the incoming rent. The investor keeps any profit above the market value of £159,950. It is the investor's risk to judge that the market will rise enough to make a profit.

3.5.5   Explaining Lease Options to Vendors

There are times when selling a property for cash is neither preferable nor possible. This is particularly the case when a property has little or no equity in it. If a seller needs to stop paying the mortgage and is in the position to move on without selling the property at below its full market value, then we can help by using an instrument called a lease option.

A lease option is a type of contract used in both residential and commercial property. The lease allows us or one of our associates, to rent the vendor's property and to become responsible for the vendors mortgage payments.

A lease option would suit the following situations:

The vendor has mortgage arrears and struggling to meet payment arrangements.

The vendor needs to move on immediately without any further mortgage commitments.

There is little or no equity in the property so the vendor has no room to manoeuvre.

The vendor does not need a large lump sum of cash immediately to move on with so he/she can afford to wait a while to achieve a higher price for the property.

The vendor may have decided to downsize and pay rent elsewhere in order to cut outgoings and use surplus monies released to pay off debts and build up funds without having to sell his house at a large discount.

Maybe through relationship break up or bereavement two people wish to get together and start a new life? They both have a house each so need to sell one. They do not need the money immediately and do not want to take a quick sale at a discounted price. To them this could be the ideal solution.

Maybe the vendors are now retired, they already have a holiday home elsewhere that is already paid for and now wish sell their home so they can move to it permanently. They do not wish to sell at a discount and do not need the money right away so a lease option answers their needs.

The vendor wants to secure a price that is as close as possible to today's full market price regardless of the state of the housing market in the future.

This service can be free for the vendor if they agree to use your nominated solicitor to represent them. He will be a specialist in the field of lease option agreements. The process takes approximately 28 days to complete.

Due to the flexible nature of a lease option, it is possible to structure it so that it can completely adapt to their particular set of circumstances. The lease option prompts the tenants in taking care of the property, as they have the intention of buying it in the future. The vendor can move out of the property without any further burden of mortgage payments. In return, the vendor grants us the right but not the obligation to purchase the property at a specific price in the future.

This is the option part of the agreement. The sale price that we agree upon is usually fairly close to today's full market price and the period to exercise the option is usually between 3 to 12 years.

During this period, apart from paying the vendor's mortgage, we or our associate become responsible for the full maintenance of the property as if we own it already.

We will carefully select and screen a potential tenant/buyer who wishes to buy the property (or yourself) in the future and carefully manage it as though it was already our own.

However, if we choose not to exercise the option to buy the property at the end of the period, the property would just be returned to the vendor, in as good a condition that it was handed over in, but most likely with improvements made to it. By that time, the vendor would have benefited from a long period of not paying the mortgage and the property may have experienced significant capital growth.

However, it is worth noting that more than 95 percent of options are exercised by us or our associates.

Conclusion:
The contracts of the lease options are sometimes very complex in nature. Our experience of lease options is that the language of the contract has to focus on the contract terms, rather than the price.

The finding of buyers for a proposed lease option would demand a considerable amount of time and investment on the part of the vendors and maybe beyond their experience.

3.5.6 Lease Options Explained for Vendors + FAQ's

For all practical purposes the Lease Option holder owns the property, in that they take all responsibility for the upkeep, the mortgage payments and letting the property + in short, any costs that might arise and any rental income. The only connection to the property the vendor maintains during the option period is the mortgage remaining in their name until the option period is over and the purchaser exercises the option to buy. At this point the mortgage is transferred in name also to the purchaser.

Below are some frequently asked questions that may help with your deal and the vendor.

3.5.7 FAQs

How long is the Lease Option period prior to final purchase?

> *The period for the lease option before final purchase can vary and is agreed in the terms of the individual lease option contract. Usually it will be between 3 and 21 years.*

Can the Lease Option holder decide not to exercise the option to buy and if so what happens then?

> *There are usually break clauses within the Lease Option Agreement at given intervals at which time the Lease Option holder can decide not to pursue the agreement. In this instance the ownership of the property simply reverts in full back to the original owner i.e. the vendor. In that case the vendor will have had the benefit of the mortgage being paid for the entire period the option has been in place. It is unlikely that the Option Holder would choose not to purchase at the end of the Option period.*

Will the lease option agreement cost me anything to set up?

> *No. All legal costs in setting up the agreement will be met by us, up to a value of £500. There should be no cost to the vendor in setting up the agreement.*

If the mortgage remains in my name, do I still have to make the mortgage payments?

> *No. Under the lease option agreement, which is a binding contract, the lease option holder has to make the mortgage payments to your lender.*

If the mortgage is still in my name then I must still own the house and am liable for its upkeep?

> *No. Under the lease option agreement, which is a binding contract, the lease option holder is responsible for the upkeep of the house and all maintenance.*

The mortgage remains in my name, therefore am I responsible for letting the property?

> *No. Under the lease option agreement, which is a binding contract, the lease option holder is responsible for letting the property should they choose to do so.*

Will I be able to secure a mortgage on another property whilst this house remains in my name?

> *Yes. Having this house in your name should not affect your ability to secure another mortgage on a different house. We can actually put you in touch with lenders who are familiar with the lease options and are happy to lend on this basis.*

If I am or plan to be on housing benefits can I claim whilst my old house remains in my name under the lease option agreement?

> *Unfortunately no you cannot. The government does not take into account the circumstances of the lease option and deems that as you are a house owner you cannot claim benefits for accommodation elsewhere unless you use a trade lawyer that will communicate with the council for you.*

What are the benefits of the lease option agreement?

> *The lease option gives you the immediate freedom to walk away from the property with no ongoing financial responsibility and at no cost. It allows the Option holder to delay the purchase until financing is more favourable. By delaying the transaction the option holder is often able to agree a price sufficient to cover the vendor's debts where otherwise a traditional immediate purchase might fall short. The agreement is formed via solicitors so that there is no doubt or confusion as to the nature of the agreement and it can be formulated and completed very quickly, within a period of weeks.*

What are the disadvantages and/or risks of the lease option agreement?

> *There are few for the vendor under the lease option agreement. In fact most of the risk is held by the Option*

holder. If the vendor for example is declared bankrupt then there is the risk the property can be repossessed and the Lease Option holder can lose the investment. Similarly if mortgage rates rise sharply effecting the mortgage repayments, then the Lease Option holder is exposed to this risk (not the vendor), as they are responsible for meeting the mortgage payments. The Lease Option holder can decide for whatever reason not to pursue the right to buy at the agreed price, thus making use of any break clause in the contract. In this instance ownership simply reverts back to the vendor. In this case the vendor simply inherits an asset which has been financed by a third party for the given period of the Lease Option - up to the point at which the break clause has been exercised.

Why bother with the Lease Option - Why not simply pursue the sale in the traditional manner?

The Lease Option is fast and easy. The Lease Option can also allow the vendor to sell when otherwise they may not be able to do so, for example due to market constraints.

In many cases the market value of the property has dropped so that there is little or no equity left in the property i.e. the mortgage is equal to, or greater than the current market value of the property. In this instance it can be very difficult to sell, particularly in a depressed market where buyers are few and are

making low offers in the face of difficult financing
conditions. Many vendors actually end up agreeing a
price below their mortgage liability simply to off-load
the property and so end up with a debt and no asset.
By pursuing the Lease Option agreement, often a price
can be agreed at the mortgage level so that the vendor
is not left with any outstanding debt. This is possible
because the actual final purchase transaction is
delayed.

Disclaimer: The information provided herein is not financial investment advice or legal advice but general property investment information. All comments are of a general nature only. Any information given does not take into account your particular financial situation, objectives or property investment needs. Each individual should satisfy themselves by independently seeking advice from an appropriate professional of the suitability or otherwise, of any comment or information given.

3.6   After you leave

You've got out of the house alive! Congratulations on your visit. Now complete the self-evaluation form and be really honest with yourself.

How did you do..? I certainly hope that you got a deal but, even if you didn't you can check over everything to 'do better' next time. There is one thing that I've noticed when 'shadowing' people, they seem to think that they did well and the vendor was the chap that wouldn't budge.

It's as important to self-evaluate if you get the deal, as it is if you don't. There is always room for improvement but, self-evaluation isn't self-criticism. Think of three things that you did right in the call and one tiny thing to improve for next time. That improvement might make the difference between a deal, or no deal next time.

4 Making it Your Business

4.1 What should I sell?

There are several ways to trade leads or deals but, let's start with the basics:

4.1.1 Leads
If you've had someone call or text so you have their details, that's called a lead. Leads have value but, as you've not done a great deal of work to gain it, a lead hasn't got a vast value. Motivated seller leads are traded for as little as £15 to those with some time and know what they are doing. Often *newbies* buy leads too, to practise with but, beware those that think a

lead is a deal. They'll be back on the phone to you to claim a refund if they don't convert it.

Beware the refund seekers – you've done your bit by dragging the lead in, you've been paid for passing it on. The strange thing when some can't convert they seem to lose their manners and professional etiquette – it's for this reason that I don't sell my leads on, I'd rather put the ones I don't want in the bin or sell them as practice leads six-twelve months later. Don't say that I didn't warn you!

Go one step further and qualify the lead. I get entries on my website that are like this:

Name: xyxyxyhrhrg

Address: rnrrntkhifid

Email: cbcbffm@djdssii.juddjd

Phone number: 07978676757474 58587676

Best time to call: yohinjbu ne

If you call the lead, you'll know that you're passing on genuine leads. If you sell junk, you'll get junk customers.

4.1.2 Qualified Leads

This takes a phone call using script two just to find out a little bit more about the lead. It's not difficult and can raise the value of your lead considerably. Qualified lead values can range from £100-£500 depending on the area, property type, and agreed deal. No paperwork is required but, photos (taken by the vendor) can help sell your lead.

No conversion has taken place, so it's still a lead.

4.1.3 Finder's Fee

This type of deal is probably my favourite. It takes a visit and paperwork to secure (as described) but, your lead is now a deal. Photos can be taken on your vendor visit and some marketing put together to advertise your deal.

I'd recommend that you take six photos of the property and these are: Kitchen, Living Room, One Bedroom, Bathroom, Back Garden and Front of House as your main ones plus any others that will enhance your marketing. Don't forget to take a shot of anything that may cause a complaint later, a fault or remedial work that may be required to your buyer.

Finder's Fee deals have a value of between £1,000-£3,000 – don't try and charge out the maximum if you're starting out, let them go inexpensively to build your reputation and then raise your prices as you develop as a *sourcer*.

4.1.4 Packaged Deals

If you have a power team in place including trade property lawyers and brokers you can offer packaged deals. You'll be able to charge more but, expect to manage the deal through to completion. This can be admin heavy work and your buyers (and vendors) will want updating on a regular basis, sometimes every day throughout the process.

Think of yourself as a match-making service between the two (vendor and buyer).You'll need decent marketing material including financial breakdowns, photos, area profile, comparables of sales and rentals and anything that will describe your deal to your audience.

4.2   Making a Brochure

4.2.1   Tips on photographing properties (rooms)

If you're a photographer with a great big Canon and a massive flash gun mounted on top, leave it at home. A vendor home is no place for a photo shoot, you'll come across more as an estate agent and we don't want that. An iPhone (other smart phones are available) is a good enough tool for the job as long as you follow a few simple rules.

Most phone cameras are of poor quality, the lenses aren't good, the flash is harsh and the photos have a 'night club' feel.

These cameras will work well if they are kept completely still. Try it for yourself, hold your phone camera on a table or any solid surface and take a shot. You'll be surprised at the quality of the shot and if you transfer that technique to your vendors house by using tables, door frames, chairs or anything that will give a solid surface, you'll come out with good looking photos.

Estate agents typically take room shots from a corner (and up high) as these shots give as much detail on the room as possible and make the room look as large as possible. You can replicate this technique by using a door frame as doors are usually at the corner of a room. Simply hold your phone tight to the door frame, angled across to the opposite, bottom corner and take the shot.

Remove any laundry or messy items from the shot before you take it. If there are flowers in the room, move them into shot to create the best look.

Okay, let's move to the 'front of house' shot. If you take a photo including the front door, there's a chance that one of your own clients will go 'wandering' and end up knocking on the door. You don't want this, even if they are totally innocent but, end up speaking with the vendor, there's a chance of them messing up the deal. Instead, take a short walk along the street and look back to your target house. Take the shot including several others but omitting the door number from your shot. We don't want to deceive anyone so do include your property but, along with some others.

It's not as easy as it seems to take good photos of homes but, if you have built some great rapport with your vendor you may decide that it's okay to take the big camera in. I've compiled some tips for you for taking some good shots for your marketing material. The big camera is for a second visit, generally not on the initial visit...

Mark's Tips:

De-clutter and clean up beforehand - items such as bottles of lotion on the nightstand, unmade beds, full rubbish bins, and raised toilet seats are distracting

Take as many photos as possible – I take as many as possible; those that know me will see my shots that I display on Facebook. Often, I've taken a couple of dozen shots, just to get the one that I want to display.

Pay attention to lighting and try not to use a flash – use a tripod if you have one. Unless you know how to use a flashgun, you'll get those flat, harsh images so often seen on social media sites of people on a night out. Flash needs to be used subtlety by bouncing off a ceiling or wall.

Try getting down on the floor and up on a chair, experiment with different angles

Take photos both of vignettes and full room shots – a wide angle lens is good for room shots, 10-22mm (Canon) is a great lens for this and the choice of countless estate agents.

Take your time and don't rush.

Don't be afraid of cropping – you can remove things that don't add to the shot or distract from your image.

Double-check the photos before using them to be sure you've chosen the best images and that they're light enough – over expose slightly when using for electronic applications such as brochures as your shot will lose a little vibrancy when compressed.

Standing back at different angles gives a room depth and dimension – Sometimes, just recomposing can alter the feel of an image and make a better shot altogether.

I think photographing rooms in natural light helps. The best light is at dawn or dusk, often called the golden hour in photography terms as the light is at its warmest. Shots taken midday will be slightly 'bluer' with a colder feel.

Compose objects so that there is breathing room – leave some space around an object to allow the eye of the viewer to wander around the frame.

When I take photos, I usually take them from every possible angle and use elements like doorways and furniture to frame the view. Sometimes the least likely angle creates the best shot

It's ok to cheat and move things around a little for the shot – you're not trying to show it like it is, you're trying to give the best impression in your shot. Some of the best photographs have a foreground and a background. What I mean by that is two things for your viewer to look at in the same shot. A table and chairs with the kitchen in the background – get the idea..?

4.3 How do I find people to sell to?

4.3.1 How Do I Sell a Deal I Have Negotiated?

We value our partners who provide us with deals, however we will only sell true genuine below market value properties on to our investor clients. So in order for one of your deals to become a ready-made deal it will need to go through our own internal checks.

If we disagree with your valuation then we will not take on the deal. Please do not take rejected deals personally - our duty lies with our investors and to make sure all the deals we offer are genuine Below Market Value Deals. Good hunting and hopefully you'll find lots of deals we can sell on, and create a WIN-WIN for everyone involved.

4.3.2 Why Pass Us Your Deals

If you have been passing deals for very long you will soon realise that selling a deal is not difficult, but getting that sold deal through to completion is the difficult part. We have painstakingly built a very efficient team of brokers and lawyers and contract chasers who together can get the sale through quickly and painlessly so that you can concentrate on what you do best which is finding more deals! And we will make sure they get sold.

4.3.3 Building an Investor/Client List

Building a client list is vital for you to have someone to sell your deals to. There are forums/groups on Facebook, LinkedIn in the online world and at least 50 property networking meetings every month. In your area there will be at least two you can visit every month.

Join the online groups, as many as you can – contribute to the discussions and get yourself known. Get out to the property events and speak with people.

Buying a list is a strategy that some use and if you choose this route be careful adding them to the mainstream email marketing companies (Constant Contact, Aweber etc.) as they will swiftly close your account and ban you if they suspect a bought list has been added.

Once you start to add contacts to your list, you'll soon realise that your ISP limits the amount of emails that you can send per day to 200-300 and this may not be enough for you to market your deals to your contacts.

If you buy a list, then it will need cleaning of bounces, duplicates and unsubscribed email addresses before you start to market to them. There's a cleaning service in the online store if you decide on this route.

The general rule for email marketing is much like property networking or speaking – don't try and pitch too hard, too soon. If you do, you'll end up with tons of unsubscribes followed by a ban. Instead send lots of useful and relevant content, make a small offer only after you have 'touched' your prospects at least seven times.

Make your content make them want to open and read your messages, keep it personal, I'm sure we've all received emails headed, Dear %firstname% - does that seem personal to you? Me neither. The bigger you get, the harder being personal will be but, you have to learn. It's beyond the scope of this book to explain but, I'll give you an idea. Click on Richard Branson on Facebook, like his page and you'll see what personal is all about. The chap runs a multi national, multi million dollar organisation and I still feel like I know him – that's being personal professionally.

CRM (Customer Relationship Management) Software

In the old days we used to use 'drop files' relating to the number of days in the month. It's arguably; the easiest, non-technical and cheapest way to track leads and it's been around for years. Another, sometimes overlooked advantage is that drop files are virtually fool proof. You take the lead details on paper; drop it into the file on the date corresponding to the follow up call you're going to make. I'd love to improve on that or say that I've come up with something better but, the reality is, there's nothing better or cheaper. We have gone all techy nowadays with our computers, software, and social media marketing but, in reality, on a limited budget, drop files work just as well.

Perhaps a more modern way to track leads is using CRM Software of which, there are plenty to choose from. I started with ACT by Sage and at £200 as a desktop application served me well for a couple of years. I then moved on to an online solution, including some expensive ones. To start with I'd stick to a free provider, learn to use CRM and develop your business from there. They never do quite what you expect them to, straight out of the box, so be ready for some phone calls to helplines and quite frustrating conversations to start with.

An example of a freebie provider is Zoho. It's a little cranky, doesn't do exactly what you'll want but, it is free as long as you have the account and works like most CRM systems. I'd advise joining their help group on LinkedIn rather than call their helpline, as most people that use it will have gone through similar issues when setting up.

I'd stay away from the more expensive systems as they'll take a good while to learn and they'll be set up for medium to large companies as opposed to a one man band. We now use, Salesforce, which is a good system but, it took me an age to learn and it's quite expensive when matched with our email marketing software. Training for a lot of software can be £100 an hour so it doesn't come cheap. Our Salesforce training was ten hours and that only got us up and running.

4.3.4 Property Networking

I'm an advocate of property networking and made the decision to 'put myself out there' during 2010 I can say with some degree of integrity that it was the best decision I made with regards to my property business. It won't suit everyone and may not suit you but, if you follow some of the guidelines below you'll be a more successful networker and grow your business in the meantime.

Property networking is an effective low-cost marketing method for developing opportunities and contacts, based on referrals and introductions - either face-to-face at meetings and gatherings, or by other contact methods such as phone and email.

Property networking is a way for you to make the maxim, "It's not what you know; it's who you know…" work for you.

The principles and techniques of property networking are mostly common sense. Many of the behavioural principles apply also to business and relationships generally, and specifically to selling, managing, coaching, facilitating, etc.

These tips apply broadly to any sort of property networking - face-to-face, organized events, business social networking websites, etc:

Ten essential principles

1. Elevator speech - Describe yourself concisely and impressively.

2. Be different - Differentiate yourself. Aim high. Be best at something.

3. Help others -Help others and you will be helped.

4. Personal integrity - Integrity, trust and reputation are vital for networking.

5. Relevant targeting - Groups and contacts relevant to your aims and capabilities.

6. Plans and aims - Plan your networking - and know what you want.

7. Follow up - Following up meetings and referrals makes things happen.

8. Be positive - Be a positive influence on everyone and everything.

9. Sustained focused effort - Be focused - and ever-ready.

10. Life balance - Being balanced and grounded builds assurance.

Describe yourself - elevator speech

Use these principles also in text-based descriptions for the web and printed materials, etc.

This is commonly called an 'elevator speech' or 'elevator pitch' - as if you were to meet a potentially important contact for the first time in an elevator at a conference and he/she asks you: "What do you do?" You have no more than 20 seconds - perhaps just 10-15 seconds - between floors to explain and to make such an impressive impact that the person asks for your contact details.

If you talk (or write) too much, the listener (or reader) will become bored, or think you are rude or too self-centred. Be concise. You will demonstrate consideration and expertise by conveying your most relevant points in as short a time as possible.

Here are the main points for creating your elevator speech:

Your name "My name is..." Look the other person in the eye. Smile. Shoulders back. Speak with confidence. Sincerity and passion are crucial in making a strong early impression.

Your business name   "I work for..." or "My business is ..." Loud clear proud again. Do not ask "Have you heard of us..?" or wait for recognition.

Based and covering where "I am based..." and "I cover..." Adapt the town, city, geography for the situation. There is little value in mentioning a tiny village if you are at a global gathering, or your global coverage if you are at a local town gathering. Make this relevant to the situation.

Your personal specialism and/or offering, and your aims. Be different and special and better in some way from your competitors. Be meaningful for the event or situation or group, and as far as you can guess, be meaningful for the contact. Express what you offer in terms of positive outcomes for those you help or supply, rather than focusing on technical details from your own viewpoint. Load your statements here with special benefits or qualities. Be positive, proud and ambitious in your thinking and expression of what you do. Include in this statement what your aims are, to show you have ambition and that you know what you are seeking from network contacts.

Depending on the situation, aim to complete your explanation in less than 20 seconds.

Less is more: lots of powerful points in very few words make a much bigger impact than a lengthy statement. It is a sign of a good mind if you can convey a lot of relevant impressive information in a very short time. Conversely, a long rambling statement shows a lack of preparation, professionalism and experience.

While you are speaking look the other person in the eyes, and be aware of his/her body language to gauge for interest and reaction to you personally, and to help your assessment of the other person's character and mood.

After your 'elevator speech' end it in a firm, positive, constructive way.

Ending with a question enables more to happen than letting the discussion tail off nowhere or into polite small-talk. Depending on the situation and visible reaction (again see body language for clues of interest) you can end in various ways, for example:

"What's your interest here/at this event?"

"What are you most wanting to get out of this event/your visit here?", or obviously if you've not already asked:

"What do you do?"

If you already know the other person's interests and motives, for example ask:

"How would you like to improve/change/grow...?

After giving your elevator speech avoid the temptation to force your business card onto the other person (unless this is the tone and expectation of the event), and certainly do not launch a full-blooded sales pitch. Instead try to develop the discussion around what the other person wants to do, achieve, change, grow, etc. And be on your guard for interruptions and sudden opportunities:

Many highly competent business people have a habit of interrupting and cutting short discussions when they see an opportunity. This means you may not always finish your elevator speech, in which case allow the discussion to progress, rather than try to complete what you planned to say.

Be prepared at any time to respond effectively to an interruption like, "Okay, I get the picture - now what exactly do you need..."

Be different and ambitious

If there is no special difference between you and other providers, people have no reason whatsoever to choose to work with you. Look again at how you describe your business offering (or yourself as a person) - what's different or special about it (or you) compared with all the others? If there is no difference, you must find a way to create one.

Sometimes this is merely a matter of redefining or placing different emphasis on what you already are and already do. This difference must be something that plenty of people will find appealing; ideally irresistible. If you are struggling to find a difference or market advantage, look at your competitors and talk to your customers, and discover what's missing and what can be dramatically improved out there. There is always at least one thing, usually more - perhaps you can bundle two or three powerful market advantages together.

This difference needs to shine out in your elevator speech, and be echoed in your subsequent discussions whenever initial interest develops towards supplying something, or putting a collaborative project together.

Aim high and big when thinking about and expressing yourself and your aims. Be realistic of course, but aim to be the best and to lead in some way, in whatever specialisms and market-place you operate. Your aims should also suggest what you are seeking from property networking- otherwise, there's no reason for you to be networking.

Property networking is not simply finding customers in one-to-one meetings and connections; it's building a strong network, helpful for your aims. Accordingly project yourself as a great networker, as well as being a great supplier or specialist. Property networkers want to work with other networkers who aim high, who have great ambitions; people who see what can be, not merely what is; and who strive for change and improvement.

These attitudes make things happen.

When you meet like-minded networkers with these attitudes, your network will grow because they'll see you can make things happen too.

Help others - give before you receive

Always prioritise helping and giving to others ahead of taking and receiving for yourself. You must give in order to receive. Be helpful to others and you will be helped in return. Networks of people are highly complex - often it is not possible to see exactly how and why they are working for you, so you must trust that goodness is rewarded, even if the process is hidden and the effect takes a while.

Use the principle of 'what goes around comes around'. You could think of this as Karma in business.

A possible explanation of how Karma (or whatever you call it) produces positive outcomes is found in the rule of 'cause and effect', or the scientific law (loosely speaking) that 'every action has an equal reaction'.

Good deeds and helpfulness tend to produce positive effects. They are usually remembered and often repaid. The giver builds reputation and trust. Referrals tend to result. Imagine yourself having lots of personal connections like this. You become known as a helpful person. Word about you spreads, and your reputation grows.

People who give are seen to have strength to give. Followers gravitate to strong giving people.

Helping others extends far beyond your personal specialism or line of work. Networking is about working within a system (of people) enabling relevant high quality introductions and cooperation's, which get great results for the participants. These enabling capabilities transcend personal specialisms.

At a simpler level, always try to ask helpful questions. These typically begin with 'what' and 'how', and address an area of interest to the other person, not you. Open questions (who, what, how, when, etc - also "Tell me about...") give the other person opportunity to speak and express their views and feelings:

Ask people:

"How can I help you?"

"What can I do for you?"

Closed questions (requiring a yes or no answer, or another single response, for example "Is this your first time here?") do not offer the other person much opportunity to talk, although at certain times a good relevant closed question can be vital for clarifying things:

"Do you mean X or Y?"

"Do you want to do X or would you prefer that I do it?"

The questioning section of the sales training guide contains many useful pointers about effective questioning techniques, from the view of helping others.

Be creative and constructive in how you regard others and how you might help them. Being defensive and making assumptions tends to limit options and growth.

For example try to see your competitors as potential allies. There is a fine dividing line between the two behaviours, and positioning too many people/companies in the competitor camp can make life unnecessarily difficult. When you talk to your competitors you will often surprise yourselves at the opportunities to work together, in areas (service, territory, sector, application, etc) where you do not compete, and even possibly in areas where you do compete. This is particularly so for small businesses who can form strategic alliances with like-minded competitors to take a joint-offering to a market and compete for bigger contracts.

Keep your integrity - build trust and reputation

Always keep your integrity.

Sometimes a situation arises which tempts us to do the wrong thing, causing harm or upset that could have been avoided.

Making such a mistake can damage personal integrity.

We are all human; mistakes happen. If you do make a mistake or wrong decision - whether it significantly undermines your integrity or not - always admits it and apologise. Failing to apologise for wrong-doing often damages a person's integrity and reputation far more than the original misjudgement itself.

We only need to think of how we view people in high and public authority, notably politicians, when they fail to take responsibility and admit their mistakes. Some integrity is lost. Do it a few times and all integrity is lost. People of low integrity sooner or later find that the only friends they have left are other people of low integrity. Significantly, integrity is vital for trust to develop. Trust is simply not possible without integrity.

Building trust is essential for growing a strong property network. Lack of trust prevents successful business networking. Certain connections are absolutely impossible to make until a very high level of trust is established. Empathy and effective listening greatly assist the process of building trust. These qualities require you to be genuinely interested in others; to listen properly, and to reflect back meaningfully and helpfully.

Following up (covered below) is also a vital feature of building trust and reputation.

You will probably know a few very solid people who always keep their commitments, and who never make a commitment which they cannot keep. Aim to be like this. Reliability and dependability are highly valued qualities in relationships, especially relationships involving referrals and recommendations, because someone's reputation is at stake.

The words 'reliable' and 'dependable' do not mean that you are always available to everyone. These words mean simply that when you say you will do something you will do it.

Seek relevant groups and connections

Identify and target groups and connections which are relevant to your aims and capabilities. The more relevant targeting of groups and contacts, then more useful your meetings and referrals will be.

Certain non-business professional people can be hugely influential in networks, and greatly trusted because of their neutrality and professional standing - educators and scientists, for example. Journalists, surgeons, and magistrates, also. There are many others. It is not easy to make connections with these people through conventional business networking, but remember that a network is not only made of business-people, and be awake to these non-commercial connections when the chance comes.

If you find that your networking is producing very low opportunities for follow up and referral, try to improve your targeting. Find different groups and methods, in other words.

A true property network is a connected system of people within which referrals and opportunities can be passed through several connections, or circulated to all those connected. Networking thus can extend far beyond simply having lots of random one-to-one meetings.

A given number of people who are connected for a reason will generally be more productive than the same number of random connections.

So don't go aimlessly after every networking opportunity which comes your way; instead try to find those meetings which already function well or have the potential to do so; and consider and decide which sort of groups and contacts will be most helpful for your aims and capabilities - ideally remembering that you need to be able to help them, as well as they should be able to help you.

Within most networks people tend to have a few close and trusted connections. Choose these, your most trusted and closest associates, very carefully. Reputations are built according to your chosen contacts, in addition to how you yourself behave.

The old expression is generally true: "You can tell a man by the company he keeps..." (Or woman of course.) So focus your efforts on groups and connections of integrity, as well as relevance.

You can identify your target group criteria in your networking strategy or plan, explained next.

Plan your networking - know what you want - manage it

All projects need managing. Property networking is a project, and so it needs managing. You can use various tools to manage your networking. You must manage your networking, or it will manage you.

Some people plan with shapes and connections on a big sheet of paper. Others prefer a spreadsheet. Use whatever you find comfortable. Be able to plan and monitor your networking activities. It is important to know exactly what you want, because you will be asked - very directly by powerful potential contacts - and you will need to give a clear answer.

An activity which has no clear planned outcomes is liable to be pulled in all sorts of unwanted directions. As with any project, you will only move towards your aim when you keep focused on that aim. If you don't know what to plan, then probably some research is necessary:

In terms of evaluating and choosing a potential networking group - especially a big online community - investigate the tactics that successful members are using. Ask a leading member for pointers. This will help you assess the group's relevance to your needs and strengths.

You will save yourself from attending time-wasting events, and registering with time-wasting websites, if you do some research before committing valuable time to deeper involvement.

A plan is vital because property networking can be a very time-consuming activity. Have some measurable targets and monitor your results. A structured approach can be especially important for very sociable networkers. Property networking can be a very enjoyable activity, and for some people can seem a lot more productive than it actually is, so stay mindful of business results and cost-effectiveness.

Here is a simple example for planning and monitoring networking, which extends the elevator speech template above. Just use the headings as a guide if you prefer to work more intuitively, or if you favour a certain type of planning method.

Property networking planner example

- What is my aim?
- Ideal connections (people) - describing words
- Group name and type
- Group profile/sector/interests (relevance to me)
- Tactical group notes/tips - what works well?
- My elevator speech (for this group)
- What I can do for these people
- What do I want from these people?
- Diary dates/scheduled tasks
- Targets/expectations
- Actuals
- Time spent
- Compare with my other marketing activities

The framework can be extended to manage specific follow-ups.

The example above doesn't necessarily suggest you begin with three groups, or limit your networking activities to three groups. A sensible start might be to pick one property meeting and one website, and one face-to-face property networking group or event, and see how you do before increasing the activity.

As you will see from the sustained focused effort point, property networking works best when it is attacked in a concentrated way. If you take on too many groups and websites at the same time you will be spread too thinly, and find it difficult to make an impact in any of them.

Follow up your commitments and promises

There are two main reasons for the importance of following up:

- Networking only produces good results when it is followed up.
- Following up with contacts builds trust, reputation, and relationships.

Put negatively, to emphasise the points:

- Networkers who meet people and never follow up are wasting their time.
- Networkers who never follow up will eventually become known as time-wasters.

Follow up is a matter of relevance and commitment: If a contact or referral is not relevant, then say so, which avoids any expectation of follow up. If there is relevance, follow it up, and in whatever way is appropriate for the situation. If you find that you do not want to follow up meetings and referrals because of lack of relevance then you can re-examine your group targeting strategy. You might be chasing the wrong groups and connections, and could need to redefine these issues.

- Be a positive influence
- Be positive. Use positive language. Smile. See the good in people.
- Be known as a really positive person. It rubs off on others and people will warm to you for being so.
- Keep your emotional criticisms of others and personal hang-ups to yourself.
- Speak ill of no-one.
- Be passionate and enthusiastic, but not emotional or subjective.
- Avoid personalising situations. Remain objective.
- Seek feedback and criticism about yourself and your ideas from others. It is the most valuable market research you can obtain - and it's totally free.
- Be tolerant. Be patient. Be calm and serene - especially when others become agitated.

Followers gather around people who remain positive and calm under pressure, and who resist the herding tendencies of weaker souls. At many networking events and situations you will have the opportunity to give a presentation to the assembled group. This is a wonderful chance for you to demonstrate your expertise in your specialist area, your positive confident character, and also to pass on some useful information.

When giving presentations in these circumstances, avoid giving a hard-selling pitch, unless you are sure that such a style is appropriate. Usually it is not. Aim to inform and educate rather than to sell. In many networking situations a strong selling presentation is regarded as insulting by those present. This is especially so if you are a guest of a group that you would not normally meet regularly.

You will sell yourself best by giving helpful information in a professional and entertaining credible manner. Be confident, positive and enthusiastic, but do not let this develop into pressure on the audience, or a sense of your trying too hard. Try to find and present within your specialism the most helpful information for the group concerned. Your aim at the end of the presentation is for the audience to have learnt something useful about your area as it applies to them, and to have been impressed with your professionalism and command of your subject.

- Apply sustained focused effort
- Property networking is a form of marketing.
- All forms of marketing benefit from strongly focused activity, which is necessary first:
- To create awareness, and then
- To build relationships to the point when a sale can be made

A given amount of effort will produce much greater results when applied consistently in a strongly focused way, than the same amount of effort spread over several wider activities, especially if spread over time too. This especially applies to property networking websites, where occasional light involvement has little impact, but focused continuous efforts can achieve a visible profile and build many connections.

The same principle applies to local meets, where occasional participation rarely penetrates the usual inner core of members, but regular enthusiastic involvement inevitably gains attention.

You should also be continuously open to unplanned networking opportunities, which can arise at any time. Business people are mostly normal human beings just like you. They have social lives, they travel, go to shops, sports events, restaurants, pubs, concerts, etc., and do lots of other things that you do too, quite outside of work. Paths can cross in the most unexpected places. You will find and develop connections in these unplanned situations if you:

- Make eye-contact with people and smile
- Take the initiative
- Start conversations
- Generally adopt an open friendly approach to everyone
- And always carry a pen and some business cards

Thereafter in all cases - planned and unplanned - much depends on what you offer to your connections.

Property networking meets and websites are full of people with many connections but little of value to offer, and they achieve poor results. Good results come instead from being friendly and open, from taking the initiative, from working hard at sustaining genuinely helpful contributions wherever you meet people.

In face-to-face networking meets there is often a 'clique culture', in which members are defensive or sometimes seemingly arrogant. This often indicates a requirement to become known and trusted, which takes time and effort. (That said, if there is genuine arrogance, you would be sensible to find a different group.) Property networking, like any other business activity, requires concentrated effort to produce results.

If you treat networking like an occasional or purely social club it will not produce good business results. Property networking requires sustained effort to make things happen.

Sustained focused effort does not mean delivering a full-blown sales pitch to every person you meet, and plastering your brochures all around the hotel lobby.

Sustained focused effort means working hard to become a regular active helpful presence in the group. Build relationships first, your reputation next, and referrals and introductions will follow.

TASK

Seek out a local property meeting in your area and make a point of attending regularly. The cost of these meets is around £15-£25 and you'll get to know the people operating in your area. What they do, what they're looking for and maybe chances to JV together.

Leave your wallet in the car for at least three meetings, as everyone is selling something (no matter what they say). Meetings are about doing business but, there's no need to jump in and buy something at your first meeting.

The speakers are making their living by giving the audience some value and content usually followed by an offer for further information if you buy.

The point is to listen, if the speaker is talking about that you may be interested in pursuing, and then have a word when they've finished their slot to find out a little more.

You have to get on with the people you choose to work with; this is a chance to see if they are your kind of person. Even then, there's still no need to buy anything. It's only the start of the relationship, please remember that.

Some speakers will only have a book, or a one day course to sell and they may pitch too hard – take it with a pitch of salt, it's only their enthusiasm that causes this. Most speakers wouldn't last long on the circuit if their product wasn't up to speed.

4.3.5   Client Marketing

To market deals to an investor client, you'll need some form of marketing material. I'd suggest a program that you're familiar with to start with. Word and PowerPoint can both produce attractive documents to make up a brochure. If you need help, there's a full PowerPoint template on the website to download. You'll be able to copy/paste pictures and information straight into the layout.

If you open a Dropbox account, the brochure can be uploaded (or saved) into your Dropbox folder which saves your audience having to wait for it to download. Dropbox provide a public link to your documents allowing fast viewing.

This can be sent to your ever expanding list of investor prospects. You can also post the link to your brochure on online groups and forums to allow maximum exposure. Please be active on those groups you join first as posting deals alone is usually frowned upon.

It's considered good practice to include the following as initial or headline details on forum/group posts

- 3 Bed Semi Detached, Pears Lane, Nottingham, NG4
- Market value - £85,000
- Purchase price - £57,000
- Finder's fee (split 50/50) - £6,000
- Below market value - 26%
- Market rent - £450

We are dealing with simple traded deals in this book with no *refurbs* required but, it's always worth noting somewhere on your marketing material to recommend a £1,500 'slush fund' for unseen remedial work needed. This will save you the hassle of a complaint later. The slush fund is for things like rubbish clearance, stained carpet renewal, or anything needed to put the property into a fit state for rent.

If you are passing a deal onto me, it's worth following these simple steps to stop your deal being rejected

4.4 What Happens when I can't do it alone!

4.4.1 Putting the Team Together

Once you've started some or all of these strategies, you'll find yourself wanting staff to take over the mundane tasks. First come the *leafleters* which are recruiting on the ground but, if you don't come across them during your research and testing phase, a simple advert in the local newspaper or job centre will suffice to get you going.

There's a simple recruitment form below to get you started

Example RECRUITMENT FORM – is available in the online store

After the *leafleters*, come the sales staff – these guys can be a bit more troublesome and will need some careful management. I know what you're thinking – I'm building a portfolio for myself here, why do I need sales staff? I'll cover their recruitment and management later…

Trading deals isn't just for those starting out, all successful investors trade deals to some degree or another. They may hide what they do through other corporate structures or through marketing agents but, we all trade deals.

If you were just thinking of keeping all of your deals, I'll guarantee you one thing – you'll run out of money. I can't predict when that will happen but, it will at some point – no matter how much you think you're starting with…

And when that happens, if you're not trading, you're a bit stuck. Let's say you're paying deposits and start with a hundred grand – that will get you into four properties with a bit of jiggling but, four properties on single lets won't replace a full time income...

Let's say that your strategy is flips, you've heard that there's big money in flips – and there is, if it's done right. Trouble is, not everyone goes right, funds get stuck in deals, financing gets pulled, and lenders change their criteria, the market changes.

A well-known company I work with has this general rule – buy three, expect to make big on one, not so big on the second and hopefully break even on the third.

No matter what 'fool proof' plan you have, you'll run out of money at some point if you just buy, and that's why we all trade. It's not a standalone strategy, it's not something we do for fun (although, it can be), we do it because it brings in cash flow and helps us save for more deposits. Trading also widens your network – what do they say? Your Network is your Net Worth...

You might consider a virtual PA to take the initial calls for you, this is recommended because it will move one step from the process and therefore help you from 'falling' into a negotiation on the phone on the initial call.

So, the team is building and you may find that you're beginning to 'buy another job' which isn't the point of trading property but, this is phase one. We do what others won't so we can enjoy later, what others can't.

I would hope by this stage you're beginning to see how Dominate Your Ground is an overall strategy to get leads on an area. Each individual strategy adds up to be greater than just the sum of the parts to create an area where your competitors can't operate and you control the area. It isn't just one strategy; it's all of them to Dominate Your Ground.

Once you've started some or all of these strategies, you'll find yourself wanting staff to take over the mundane tasks. First come the *leafleters* who are recruited on the ground but, if you don't come across them during your research and testing phase, a simple advert in the local newspaper or job centre will suffice to get you going.

A morning briefing, issuing of 'doors' and equipment is a vital part of recruitment and on-going management. If you recruit on the ground you'll find those that are already doing the job for someone else, they will be used to the leg work, the hours and the weather.

The weather for us that work in offices is a strange thing. If you currently work in an office, go a day out to the races, or a sporting event on a spring or autumn day. You may be shocked how cold it actually is outside for periods of longer than a few hours. New leaflet recruits often haven't been 'weathered' so beware the guy that comes from a 'warm' work place into this type of work.

I must confess that I'm a bit sexist when it comes to leaflets, not because of a deep routed personality disorder; it's just that the girls always seem to do it better than the boys (younger ones). The older guys can be quite good, especially an ex postie or dog walkers, these guys have been weathered too.

People do what's inspected, not expected – it may be useful to bare this phrase in mind.

If you don't manage your staff, you'll have no business and I mean manage on the ground. Meet them on their rounds; greet them with a chocolate bar and a bottle of water. Heaps of praise, and let them know that you'll be staying in the area for the day.

The tips above (if you do them) will instantly double your call rate. I'll guarantee that and I know it because I've measured it countless times. I get double the amount of calls when I deliver my own leaflets – funny that...

If you're starting off with some funds behind you, then you might have considered using Royal Mail. Check out their website and click on the Door to Door Service for more details. They'll charge around double what you'd by paying your leaflets guys and that's for a multi drop not a solus (lots of leaflets together).

I'll say this as plainly as I can – if you pay double the rate for a multi drop, the chances are that you don't care too much about the skill of marketing and haven't time to waste on managing your area – I'll put my neck out and say that you'll get a few calls and give up fairly early on. That's just what I've found from experience, no real numbers or science behind my statement. Those that I find, care about their areas seem to do better.

If you care about your ground, it will return the care back to you in deals.

Secondly, it's the 'bin stick' guys and the same general rules apply with these. Also recruited from the ground, briefed and managed in the same way.

4.4.2   Growing Your Property Business

This section is based around your management of staff as you grow, although at this point, you may think – I'm going to remain a one man band – take this section, 'just in case'

There are seven S's of Sales Management and I'll go through them for you. They are taken from a Japanese management strategy that included three hard S's and four soft S's. The three hard S's are strategy, structure and systems.

Strategy places emphasis on a sales persons and sales managers need for a chartered course of action, the practice of good time management, and the allocation of resources and removing the barriers to trading.

The assignment of sales territories, quotas, training, presentations and coaching on the correct way to establish sales visit agendas.

Structure refers to the way that you set up your organisation, the hierarchy, the relationship with staff and support, and how the sales cycle works.

More difficult are the four soft S's and you should emphasise these the most. These represent personal concern, caring for one another and human investment. The soft S's are staff, style, skills and superordinate.

Staff is the demographic description of personnel categories within your organisation such as area manager, representative, branch manager and although these positions appear to be perfunctory, in successful companies, in line with the Japanese model, are treated with honour, trust and respect.

Style is the characteristic way of how key managers behave in achieving your company's goals. A strong employee company exhibits a caring attitude and helps to build trust and respect among its people and managers. The company would believe in the importance of each person within it, and their potential contribution. Managers encourage support, listening, employee involvement and participative management.

Skills represent your company's willingness to invest in adequate training for each employee's assignment. Frequently company's invest in their representatives training and omit their managers training in the art of managing people. This can result in poor supervision, and high staff turnover.

The luxury of assuming that a good sales person will make a good manager without real training has been refuted many times.

Superordinate goals have a significant meaning, since they are the guiding concepts. A hard-nosed salesperson may scoff at inspirational overtones or with sharing values of others within your company, yet, superordinate goals are one of the most important S's in successful companies.

Some managers tend to focus on the three hard S's to achieve the company's goals as these can be quantified with logic ie. Sales results tables, number of calls made, number of qualified leads – often called KPI's or Key Point Indicators. Have you heard a sales managers ask, "So, what have we sold today?"

The three soft S's are a lot harder to quantify with logic but, can be interpreted by a sales person as the caring and respectful attitude and the willingness of your company to support.

Successful sales managers feel for and with their people, consult with them, and genuinely lead by supporting them. A successful sales person's relationship with a customer is to inform, educate and to enlighten in order to make a sale.

Why would it be different for the sales manager when dealing with their own people? Instead of "So, how much did we sell today?" how about, "How can I help you to be more productive?"

The major strength of a company lies with, not in it's perfect strategies, but in its well-trained and motivated people.

4.4.3 Systems to Put in Place – Trading as a Sole Trader or Ltd. Co.

To start with you may decide that you're building a portfolio of property for yourself, and that's fine. When you finally decide that it's a business you'll need to set up a limited company or LLP Partnership to offset your expenses against tax bills. Setting up a ltd. Co. isn't difficult and can be done by nearly all accountants or online. The only real difference is that online is much cheaper but, you won't get a fancy wallet for your formation.

Register with an accountant if you're trading deals, that doesn't need to be a property accountant, it could be a business accountant.

Introduce yourself to some 'trade' lawyers and by trade, I mean property lawyers that are already in the business. Let them know what you're doing and if they could assist. There are plenty around and they would all welcome the business. If you need recommends, give me a shout.

Next step is to find a broker, an independent broker to act on your 'buying' clients behalf. Have a few in reserve so you (or your clients) don't get stuck if you need a quick decision and one's busy.

4.4.4 Outsourcing – Who Does What?

You may find that there are 'mundane' jobs that need doing that begin to sap your time. These could be making up brochures, building spreadsheets, logos, and adverts for social media or email marketing. These tasks can be outsourced to the Philippines, Elance, Guru, PPH (People per Hour) and other sites that carry out business tasks on a job by job basis or more permanent rate.

Keep your wits about you when using free lancing websites; there are just as many poor workers as there are good ones. If you start with a small job, go through the process, let them complete, see how they communicate and perform, check that it's done in the timeframe they say it will be and one budget.

Then try a slightly larger job – these initial jobs should be non-critical for you and if they mess up, you're not going to be pulling your hair out.

Think of them as assessment jobs or interview jobs – that's the way I keep my sanity in place and my jobs on schedule and budget.

There's a whole skill to outsourcing properly and when you're ready I'll gladly put you in touch with some that manage their outsourcing and help others to do the same.

4.4.5 Organisations to Consider

Once you've decided that you have a business and set up as a Ltd. Co. there's a couple of organisations to consider. First of all, get yourself some Professional Indemnity insurance to cover you for advice that you may give. It's not cheap but, it will save you in the long run. Court can be an expensive business and not to be taken lightly. If you're in business you'll see a courtroom at some point.

Now you've got all of the requirements to join The Property Ombudsman, and you can state publically, that you have a redress scheme should things go wrong for your client. The cost of membership isn't expensive and can be a unique selling point to distinguish you from your competitors.

You'll have to do things in the order set out above as they are in order of qualification for the next step...

If you are dealing with BMV Deals, Lease Options or Instalment Contracts by yourself, you'll need to obtain a CCL (Consumer Credit Licence) – this is because you will be giving financial advice and that advice is a regulated activity.

If you haven't applied for one, which is £1,200 – then you'll have to use a debt management company that has one to stay on the right side of the regulation.

When we start in business, the expenses seem a lot but, this is a business, you're not sorting out debts for a friend, you're not doing this for free – this will be your profession and professional work comes with responsibilities.

Not doing any of the above steps won't land you in jail but, could easily get you investigated by the FCA or the Office of Fair Trading. Just a word of warning, nobody wants to be investigated by a body with virtually unlimited funds. The investigation alone could put you under as they tend to be admin heavy as do VAT investigations.

If you source and trade a few deals it won't be long before you go over the VAT threshold and be forced to register. VAT investigation insurance is recommended for the same reasons. Consider this – you're a one man band that's sold 20 deals in a year at £5k each. You've paid your company taxes; you've paid your VAT bill. An investigation can put so much work on your shoulders that you struggle to concentrate on your core business.

Do your own research, ask the people that witness this, the accountants (business, not property) and see for yourself.

If you go under, that's not the end of it – your creditors will continue to chase and they can be harsh and ruthless when it comes to money.

I'm not saying don't take any chances, all businesses and entrepreneurs take chances – just don't take them all.

4.4.6 Coaching Staff to achieve Great Vendor Visits

As you grow, you may wish to use to take on staff to carry out your vendor visits. They'll need coaching to be successful, that means using a four step teaching model:

- Explanation (the knowledge)
- Demonstration (how to apply the knowledge)
- Imitation (skill)
- Consolidation (practice)

This is a continuous process and many companies fail to train their staff properly because they adopt superficial policies on training. To be successful in your company, apply the following: The three R's of training – Repetition, Reinforcement and Recognition.

Repetition – Attitudes, skills and knowledge (ASK) must be repeated to be remembered. This works on the mind much like advertising. Repeated messages are learnt, and once learnt are actioned successfully.

It is clear that a single training programme or coaching event will produce little learning but, repeated events will succeed. Good coaches constantly repeat messages in training with role plays, quizzes and discussion. (Creating unconscious competence).

Reinforcement. This is the prime role of field, or on-the-job training usually termed coaching. Observation and job related practise of ASK encourages learning by doing and reinforces the message in real life situations.

Recognition. Successful ASK progress should be recognised and rewarded motivationally by recording progress and relating development to personal growth and a career plan.

Coaching is a great excuse to develop these skills using random visits as a live vehicle. It is also a prime motivational opportunity, so try to build praise, not criticise.

Coaching reinforces off-the-job training, so use a selling model which is consistent and can be learned by repetition/practice. I've included one in the book, feel free to copy it.

Coaching must develop how, not just what. I'll explain that, it won't help much to say, "Work on your closing techniques." (what). Show how to do by using role plays (very powerful), projects, discussion and mini quizzes. Vary each method of learning to create interest.

Coaching aims to change behaviour. At the end of end coaching session, the key question is: Will the trainee change behaviour as a result of the session? This will not happen if you take over the visit or 'show off' – sometimes you must risk losing the deal to review later and change behaviour.

Before the vendor visit, always plan with the trainee and practice by mini role play and discussion – this reinforces learning.

Always move quickly from the observed visit to the skills to be developed – do not analyse specific observed situations too extensively, they are just leads. Instead concentrate on skills to be developed – even if you lost the deal.

Focus on a specific area to be developed for each coaching visit, and do not try and cover a lot of different skills as this will learning harder. Ask your trainee about their priorities for learning, question openly, and don't tell. If you don't impose your views, you'll be pleasantly surprised to find that they may be already in line.

Always end on an uplifting note to a session, summarising on strengths, progress made and action points before the next coaching event. There is little to be gained from a full 'word by word' account document.

I've included a tabled skills record which you are welcome to use – the Excel version is available from the online store

4.4.7 The Steps to Pass Us Your Negotiated Deals

Step 1 – Research – Once you have a deal you need to make sure that it stacks up.

The instructions on 'How to Value a Property' in the store will help you to determine the value of the property.

We have also included a calculator in the online store with instructions on how to use to it. This will help you with some basic number crunching i.e. the amount the lender will give depending on the rental and also the below market value percentage of the property.

Step 2 – 20% + Below Market Value – You need to make sure the deal is genuinely 20% or more below market value in order for us to take on your deal.

Step 3 – Email Us Deal Details at deals@markianson.com – In order for us to take on the deal we will need the following:

- Property address and description
- Market value of property

- Agreed purchase price
- Pictures if you can get them

We will do our own checks to see if the deal stacks up before we decide to take it on. If we are happy with the deal we will email you within 24hrs and ask for you to return a signed option agreement.

Step 4 – Option Agreement –Instructions in how to fill this in are provided with the document. There is a blank option agreement in the store.

We will do our own checks to see if the deal stacks up before we decide to take it on – I've said this twice on purpose...

Step 5 – Signed Option Agreement – Get agreement signed by vendor. Please include a fax header with your name, contact details, property description and vendors name and contact number.

Alternatively you can scan in the above and send to deals@markianson.com

Step 6 – Market Deal – We will market and sell deal onto our investor clients.

Step 7 – Arrange Mortgage – We will arrange a mortgage for the buyer.

Step 8 – Arrange Valuation – We will arrange for the survey to be carried out at the property. If the deal does not value as stated we will either try to re-negotiate the deal or return the buyers valuation fee.

Step 9 – Instruct Solicitors – We will then instruct both the buyers and vendors solicitors. The vendor's solicitor can be instructed much earlier if needed.

Step 10 – Chase Contracts –We will chase all the solicitors, broker's buyers and the vendors to make sure that completion takes place as quick as possible.

Step 11 – Receive Payment – On completion we will receive payment from our investor and then pay you 50% (inclusive of VAT) of our fee. An invoice will be required in order to pay you your monies.

TASK

Book, and attend a one day property course. The reason for this is that you'll spend around £200 for a day's training which isn't expensive. Try and pick a one day that helps your chosen strategy but, it's not that important at this stage. What's more important is seeing how the days are laid out, what to expect and how an upsell is done.

Accept that you're not going to be an expert in a day, and go along for the ride – make it a birthday present to yourself if you have to justify it.

On a one day course, you'll get as much value during the coffee breaks. They'll be people at the same level as you on

---

their journey, and the chance to meet, chat, exchange business cards is invaluable in my opinion.

Even if you think the subject matter isn't for you currently, it won't be a waste because I can guarantee you that your strategy will change throughout your journey as you learn more.

There will be an upsell.

The reason for the upsell is that it's impossible to be an expert in one day on any subject. The course host wouldn't be doing you any favours; in fact they'd be doing you a disservice if they didn't offer you the chance of further training.

Most course runners/hosts have many years' experience in their particular speciality, they take the good bits, the value bits and some of the horrors to put together a day course, as a taster.

To find out more detail on the strategy, next comes the weekend residential, or the webinar mentoring, or the three day – each host will offer something slightly different to suit their business.

If you consider the one day course as the interview for the host – if he passes the interview then go for some more training with them. That's of course, if it's your chosen strategy..!

Another great benefit of a one day is that it can sell you out of taking it further – some see a strategy mentioned a lot and you might think that it's for you. Once you're sat in a room doing a one day, you may find that it's not something you thought and it doesn't appeal – that's fine too, you just saved yourself several thousand pounds by going and finding out.

4.5 Looking After You!

4.5.1 Joining Instructions – Mentoring

I take on a limited number of clients for an initial days mentoring. I'm quite selective and we'll have to have a chat on the phone first. It's during this conversation that I gauge whether you'll 'do it' or not. I'm not looking to mentor those that can't as most of the ones that 'do' become my suppliers, and we can make some more money together.

There's a fee for my one day mentoring (changes from time to time), and that's 'hurt money' – there's no need to pay upfront but, there needs to be some 'hurt' on your part for me to consider you.

The fee isn't to make money as we all make lots more from doing deals but, I don't want to spend my time mentoring those that just fancy having the information. I'm always looking for 'doers'.

If you'd like to choose a hotel that's close to you, I'll meet you (and your partner) there. I look forward to hosting you on your day of coaching, and it will be a packed day. There are a couple of things below that would make the 28 days after you've attended, easier.

Although I help people to start patches all over the UK, it is best advice to start with a patch that's close to home. This enables you to put your systems in place before moving on to bigger things. With that in mind, please pop into a Waterstones (or WH Smith) and grab a couple of maps.

MAPS

In the UK, we have one of the best mapping organisations in the world (Ordnance Survey) and they can be of fantastic value to you.

The maps you'll be looking for are the Ordnance Survey Explorer Maps (Orange) - Don't worry, I'll show you how we are going to use them on the day.

Please ignore AA Maps, AtoZ and any other types of road map as these aren't up to the job.

NEWSPAPERS

Also, please bring with you all of the newspapers that are delivered in your area, paid and free. This will establish the competition in your area. We'll be calling a couple to demonstrate that you have nothing to fear from your competition.

USEFUL ITEMS

Calculator, notepad, laptop (internet connected), and a big smile

Save your biggest, burning questions for the ice breaker session first thing. I look forward to seeing you

4.5.2 Avoid procrastination by training yourself to act in response to do it now!

People, who procrastinate, miss things, they may be late for an appointment, they may miss a train, but more importantly they may miss an opportunity that could change their lives for the better. You may recall the story of the Babylonian trader and his camel. They both travelled with a wealthy caravan. One night the temperature dropped, it became cold and the camel begged the traveller to warm his nose - only his nose in the trader's tent.

Can you guess what happened? Little by little the camel inched in his head, his shoulders, his front legs, first one hump and then the other until finally he took over the entire tent. The trader was left out in the cold. This is exactly the same way in which procrastination can inch its way into our lives. Every time we procrastinate or put off until tomorrow what we can do today, it creeps up on us it takes over a large part of our life. Three familiar words are required DO IT NOW! Getting more things done, becoming an action person who makes use of every opportunity does not require the memorisation of some complex system; it simply requires relentless determination to ACT in response to DO IT NOW! And keep this up over a long enough period of time to make it a habit - an automatic reflex.

Perhaps the most overlooked application of DO IT NOW! Is the relation to our own ideas. We all have certain timidity towards ideas we think of ideas are personal things, part of the person who gives them birth. Most of us treat criticism of our ideas in the same way that we treat criticism of ourselves. Those of us who might otherwise be creative tend to remain silent for fear of this criticism. DO IT NOW! Gets us into action before we have time to think about possible criticism.

Make each hour count

If we make each hour count, then day-by-day, each week, each month counts. An hour in our life is like a single brick in the building of a house. A house consists of thousands of bricks but each one carries part of the load and makes up part of the appearance of the finished structure. If we make each hour count, we will build an outstanding business.

Have the phrase: "What am I doing NOW to get a deal" on a card where you will see it often.

Convert excess tension relieving time into goal achieving time

Consider how the hours during the day are broken down. They fall into two distinct areas of activity. The first is goal achieving: the second is tension relieving. Goal achieving is the time we spend progressively moving towards our goal, moving through the particular stages of our plan. Tension relieving is the relaxation, the unwinding that each of us needs every day, but we only need so much of this unwinding to recover from the stress and strain of daily life. Any excess is waste and we want to be a success, it is this "excess" which we must transfer into goal achieving time.

When that "I'm swamped" feeling creeps up on us and threatens to destroy our day, stop and say:

"I can get everything done quickly, by simply planning my work and working my plan."

I'm not saying it's going to be easy, I'm saying it's going to be worth it...

4.5.3 Next Steps

You made it this far and you've either sold yourself out of making this your business or you're dying to know more. Well, if you've sold yourself out, then I guess I won't be hearing from you soon.

If you're prepared to make sacrifice, work hard and secure a great future for yourself and your family then, read on.

To be a mentee, you'll have to attend a property networking meeting that I'm speaking at or a workshop I'm running first. The reason for this is simple – this will be my interview, you'll find out if you'd like to work with me. I'm quite direct and certainly not for everyone. I'm afraid that I don't the high fives or the mega upsell or fluff.

As you've probably gathered from the book, I try to tell it straight. If you lose focus, I'll put you back on track. If you decide on a different route, that's fine, I'll point you in the right direction. I'll take you from where you are to where you want to be.

I look forward to meeting you all, I travel up and down the country speaking at various events, shows and meetings. Don't be shy, come over and say hi – because I was where you are, once.

If you'd like to apply for mentoring, it's a simple application form and 'pay as you go' with no contracts to sign.

Have a discussion with your 'life' partner first, then give me a call for an informal chat. Your partner can attend too, and it's worth them coming to keep them on board and support you during your journey. There is no charge for them.

5   Appendix

Here are a few extra useful documents that I hope you will find interesting and useful. There are also a lot of other useful documents on my website.

Please visit me at www.markianson.com

A1. The 32 'Deal Making' Questions

Questioning Skills

Asking good questions is an art form. Property people often do all the talking and seldom ask enough questions. So if you've ever had that dry up feeling and can't think where to go with your leading questions?

Well, here they are – this takes practice, there's no need to memorise them, and they can't be scripted but, if you know them, you'll be way ahead of your competition.

1) What is your main objective? When you understand what your vendor is trying to achieve, you can match your proposal.
2) How do you plan to achieve that goal? You may already fit their plan and not even know it. If you're part of their plan, you're vendor will close themselves.
3) What is the biggest problem that you currently face? If you can help them solve their biggest problem, you will be their best friend.
4) What other problems do you experience? You may not be able to solve their biggest problem, so what other problems do they have that you can solve?
5) What are you doing currently to deal with this?
6) What is your strategy for the future? This will give you an outline of the vendor's strategy and thinking.

7) What other ideas do you have? Used to accelerate the decision making process

8) What role do others play in creating this situation? This fills in the blanks; anyone who is contributing to the problem is a potential adversary. Find out who they are.

9) Who else is affected? Anyone who is affected by the problem is a potential ally.

10) If you could have things any way you wanted, what would you change? People are naturally resistant to change. "Better the devil you know than one you don't." This question inoculates the issue of change. It also allows them to dream and explore the possibilities. You can probably do about half of the things they wish for. There is something special about making a person's dreams come true.

11) What effect would this have on the present situation? This question brings the dream to reality.

12) What would motivate you to change? This question creates the rationale they will use to justify the change, reducing the resistance later.

13) Do you have a preference? If they do, you need to know what it is and what it is based on.

14) What has been your experience? If they have had an unfavourable experience with a competitor, you may be able to exploit it.

15) How do you know? Sometimes they really don't know. You want to know where they got their information. Be very careful with the tone: you don't want to sound off hand.

16) Is there anything else that you'd like to see? This open ended question encourages them to brainstorm additional options and may reveal additional opportunities for the astute.

17) How much would it be worth to you to solve this problem?

18) What would it cost, ultimately, if things remained as they are?

19) How do you plan to finance it? Their future, where is the money going to come from? Can you offer alternative financing?

20) What alternatives have you considered? They are talking to the competition. It is perfectly appropriate to ask a prospect who the competition is. You'll know how to present your offering in the best light against your competitor.

21) What benefits would you personally realize as a result? People do things for their reasons, no matter how good your reasons might be.

22) How would others benefit? The answer to this question creates a justification for what may ultimately be a selfish decision.

23) How can I help? Easily the most powerful question in the book.

24) Is there anything that I've overlooked? This gives you a chance to tie up any loose ends that might tangle and trip you up later on down the line.

25) Are there any questions that you'd like to ask? Encourage your prospect to get all their questions answered here and now.

26) What do you see as the next step? The vendor may tell you what to do to advance the deal. Write up a contract? Check on a few points? Or nothing?

27) Who else, besides yourself, will be involved in the decision making process? Even if you're meeting with all of the owners always assume that they may be a behind the scene influencer. Even if you think you've found a decision maker, keep asking this question of everyone else.

28) On a scale of one to ten, how confident do you feel about doing business with us? What would it take to get that up to ten? This two-part question will tell you what incremental evidence they need and what form of proof they will require. If they say, "8," then say, "what would it take to get a 9?" If they say "10," then proceed to write the paperwork up.

29) Are you working against a particular deadline?

30) How soon would you like to start? These are all timeframe questions. Remember, if they are not motivated by some time frame, they probably will not buy into your deal, at least not for a while.

31) When should we get together to discuss this again? Let them define the time frame for the next meeting. If they resist, ask, "How about if I call again within the next four weeks?"

32) Is there anything else you'd like for me to take care of? We leave too much money on the table, because we do not ask this simple parting question

A2. Option To Buy Property Agreement

This Agreement is made on the _____2013

Between

1)   (the "Buyer"): and

2)   (the "Seller").

WHEREAS:

The Seller now owns (address of property)
(the "Property")

NOW IT IS HERBY AGREED as follows:

1) In consideration of the sum of £xxxx (xxxx), (the "Option
    Payment") receipt of which is hereby acknowledged by the
    Seller upon execution of this agreement, the Seller grants
    to the Buyer the exclusive option to buy the Property for
    the following price and on the following terms (the
    "Option"):

Purchase price £   (amount in words)

2) The Option Payment will be credited against the purchase price of the Property if the Option is exercised by the Buyer.

3) If, after signing this Agreement, the Seller fails to complete the sale of the Property to the Buyer, the Seller will reimburse the Buyer with all the costs that the Buyer has incurred including the Option Payment.

4) The Option Period will be for two months from the date of this Agreement ("the Option Period"). The Option shall be exercised by the service of written Notice by the Buyer on the Seller at any time within the Option Period.

5) Upon the service of the written Notice from the Buyer to the Seller exercising the Option this Agreement shall constitute a Contract for the Sale and Purchase of the Property with the terms and conditions hereunder provided.

   i. The standard Conditions of sale (Forth Edition) shall apply and are incorporated herein save that this Option Agreement is assignable.

   ii. Vacant possession of the Property will be given on completion.

   iii. The Seller shall transfer with Full Title Guarantee.

   iv. The Seller confirms that they are the registered owner of the Property and is able to sell the Property free from encumbrances.

   v. The Seller agrees not to apply for any mortgages or secured loans on the Property at any time during the Option Period.

6) If the Option is not exercised within the time herein provided the Option herein granted shall be null and void and the Seller will retain the Option Payment.

7) No modification of this agreement will be effective unless it is in writing and is signed by both the Buyer and Seller. This agreement binds and benefits both the Buyer and Seller and any successors. This document, including any attachments, is the entire agreement between the Buyer and Seller and shall be governed by English Law.

_____

Signed by or on behalf of the Seller

_____

Signed by or on behalf of the Buyer

A3. TLA - Three Letter Acronyms for Property

Compiled from all contributions on the BMV Deals & Discussions Facebook Forum

By Julie Hogbin (on 15 August 2012)

A	AS - Assisted Sale APR - Annual Percentage Rate ASA - Advertising Standards Authority AST - Assured Short Hold Tenancy - The agreement between the landlord and the tenant ARLA - Association of Residential Letting Agents AT - Assured Tenancy (agreement)
B	BC - Borough Council BI - Buildings Insurance BMV - Below Market Value BMRV - Below Mortgage Redemption Value BOE - Bank Of England BS - Building Society BTL - Buy To Let BTS - Buy To Sell
C	Contracts - The agreement set between two parties to buy/sell/lease/rent a property CAGR - Compound Annual Growth Rate CC - County Council CCJ - County Court Judgement CGT - Capital Gains Tax, a tax on the profits on a sale (currently 40% normally) CH - Central Heating COCR - Cash On Cash Return. CPO - Compulsory Purchase Order CT - Council Tax

D	DD - Due Diligence - The process through which a potential buyer evaluates a property for acquisition. (PPPPPPP – pre planning prevents pretty poor performance) DD (2) - Direct Debit DG - Double Glazing DIP - Decision in Principle DPC - Damp Proof Course DPM - Damp Proof Membrane DSCR - Dept Service Coverage Ratio. DSS - Department of Social Security DTI - Department of Trade and Industry
E	EA - Estate Agent EDC - Exchange with a Delayed Completion EDMO - Empty Dwelling Management Orders EPC - Energy performance certificate grades the energy efficiency of a property and is mandatory in any sale or let. Also a housing stealth tax ERC - Early repayment charges E&OE - Errors and Omissions Excepted
F	F - Freehold- Ownership of property in perpetuity, or until sale, as against Leasehold where the property is owned for the period of the lease following which it reverts to the Freeholder Finance - Lifeline of any property deal. FLEA - Fire, Lightning, Earthquake, Aircraft (insurance) FR- fixed rate FSA - Financial Services Authority (now FCA) FSS - Full Structural Survey FTB - First Time Buyer FCA – Financial Conduct Authority
G	GCH - Gas Central Heating GDV - Gross Development Value GFCH - Gas Fired Central Heating GP - Gross Profit GR & NR - Gross & Net Return GRQ - Get Rich Quick GY - Gross Yield, the annual rent as a percentage of the cost or value of the property

H	HA - Housing Authority HB - Housing Benefit HHSRS - Housing Health and Safety Rating System HIPS - Home Information Packs HMO - house of multiple occupancy - licensed and unlicensed HPI - House Price Index HR - Home Report, sellers must have a Home Report prior to presenting their property to the market (Scotland Only) It includes: Property Questionnaire Single Survey Report and Valuation Energy Performance Certificate Mortgage Valuation Report HMRC - Her Majesty's Revenue & Customs
I	IC - Instalment Contract IFA - Independent Financial Advisor IO - Interest only: A mortgage where capital debt is held off until the end of the term. Interest payments to service the debt are made at regular periods. IR - Inland Revenue IRR - Internal Rate Retention / Internal Rate Of Return ISA - Individual Savings Account
J	JV - Joint Venture ....Typically a percentage share of the upsides (and any downsides) and not to be confused with a loan by a third partner. Easiest way to think of a JV is Dragons Dens Arrangement typically on a property by property basis, and like Dragons Den - the percentage split can be anything that works for both 50/50 70/30 80/20 etc JVP - Joint Venture Partner
K	KFI - Document mortgage broker provides stating repayment terms etc and 'key facts' K.P.I. - Key Performance Indicators - Measure everything. It's the road to improvement
L	LA - letting agent OR local authority LHA - Local Housing Authority LL - Landlord LO - Lease Option LTB - Let To Buy LTV - loan to value. LTV Ratio or LTV %, or loan-to-value, is how much mortgage/loan you have in relation to how much your property is worth. A ratio to which a lender will fund a purchase

M	MAP - Mortgage Agreement in Principle
	MH - Mortgage Host – using a partner (that can get lending) to buy a
	     property, your interest secured with a Deed of Trust
	MIG - Mortgage Indemnity Guarantee
	MIP - Mortgage Indemnity Premium
	MV - Market Value. The price that a property is valued at based on
	     comparable properties, market conditions and a price of the
	     property which is the highest price a buyer is likely to pay and the
	     lowest price a vendor is likely to sell for

N	NAEA - National Association of Estate Agents NALS - National Association of Letting agents NEG - Negotiable NHBC - National House Building Council Scheme NLA – National Landlords Association NI - National Insurance NMD - No Money Down - The art of buying a property then remortgaging it for the same NP – Net Profit NPV - Net Present Value
O	OCH - Oil Central Heating ODPM - Office of the Deputy Prime Minister OFCH – Oil Fired Central Heating OFT - Office of Fair Trading OIEO - Offers In Excess Of OIRO - Offers In the Region Of OMV - Open Market Value OO - Owner Occupier OP - Original Poster OPM - Other People's Money: Using other people's money to purchase properties OTO – Open to offers
P	PA - Per Annum / Personal Assistant PCM - Per Calendar Month PI - Professional Indemnity (insurance) P&L - Profit & Loss POA - Price On Application PP - Planning Permission PP - purchase price PPPPPP – pre planning prevents pretty poor performance PPR - Principle Private Residence

Q	QE - Quantitative Easing: government conjuring money out of thin air to encourage spending? QL - Qualified Lead - Vendor has been contacted and a certain level of motivation to sell the property has been determined and that information is now being sold.
R	R&D - Research And Development R&M - Repair and Maintenance RI - Rental Income RICS - Royal Institute of Chartered Surveyors ROE - Return On Equity ROI - Return On Investment ROR - Rate Of Return RP - Redemption Penalty RPI - Retail Price Index RR - Rent Review RT - Regulated Tenancy (agreement)
S	SARB/SRB - Sale and Rent Back SB - Scum Bag tenant who doesn't pay! SD – Stamp duty SDLT - Stamp Duty Land Tax SO - Standing Order SSTC - Sold Subject To Contract SSTCM - Sold Subject To Concluded Missives STC - Subject To Contract STR - Sell To Rent SV-surveyor valuation SVR - Standard Variable Rate - Mortgage
T	TA - Tenancy Agreement TBA - To Be Agreed TDS's. - Tenancy Deposit Scheme's TR- tracker rate
U	
V	VAT – Value added tax
W	WACH – Warm air central heating
X	
Y	
Z	

C3 - family home

C4 - shared house (3 or more sharers)